Strictly from Hungary

Ladislas Farago

Introduction by John Farago

WESTHOLME

Westholme Publishing

904 Edgewood Road

Yardley, Pennsylvania 19067

www.westholmepublishing.com

ISBN 978-1-59416-006-6

Also available as an eBook.

Printed in the United States of America.

Dedication

To the memory of MY MOTHER, who used to forgive me worse things than this

LADISLAS FARAGO, NEW YORK, 1962

This new edition is dedicated to my father's brother, PAUL FARAGO. For as long as I knew him, Paul exhorted those around him, in his impossible-to-place Anglo-European accent, to pay no attention to the Hungarian behind the curtain. And yet after six decades of life in Australia he still seemed wistfully at home strolling Andrássy út in 2002. Sadly, Paul died as this book was going to press.

Among contemporary and future Hungarians, the dedication goes first to my son MAX, just discovering his central European soul at age 18. I wish him many years of the sweetest paprika, the fattest goose livers, and the highest octane barack palinka. To my wife JEANNE MARTIN, who has embraced my Hungarian dream with the don't-look-back enthusiasm of a native Magyar, and to our friend and Budapest mentor, ELIANE PICKERMANN, who demonstrates daily that *joie de vivre* is how "Hungarian" is spelled in French.

JOHN FARAGO, BUDAPEST, 2004

Preface

I accept full responsibility for every word in this book, but I would like to acknowledge my debt of gratitude to my friends Imre Kelen, Sandor Incze, Miklos Lazar, Si Bourgin, Georges Mikes, Eugene Fodor, Jay Nelson Tuck, Sidney Shelley, and especially the late Ferenc Molnar and Ferenc Gondor, who allowed me to draw upon their memories.

Every story in this book is true (more or less) but most of the names had to be doctored.

LADISLAS FARAGO, NEW YORK, 1962

This new edition of *Strictly from Hungary* is, of course, a labor of many loves. Bruce Franklin, a modern visionary with the prescience to look backward while moving forward, has been the *sine qua non*. Kúnos László and Bart István were also essential to the success of the effort. Those who have helped build the bridge between my father's Budapest and mine include: Bakos Anita, Biro Csaba, Kerekes Aniko, Torok Andras, and Tercsak Tamas.

But the Budapest of this book has more ethereal roots as well: In family—Lisa, Richard and Nick Farago—in shades of my youth— Sandor Ince, Imre and Betty Kelen, Alex King, Gene and Vlasta Fodor, Albi and Marika Frankel, George Lang and August Molnar. Those roots flourished in a Budapest-in-New York that has all but vanished: the old Budapest Restaurant (my favorite among the dozens that crowded Yorkville forty years ago), Rigo Pastry, Paprikas Weiss' astonishing emporium, and, among the stalwart survivors, Orwasher's Bakery and the restaurant Mocca.

JOHN FARAGO, BUDAPEST, 2004

Contents

How I Came
to be
Strictly from Hungary

On July 20, 2003, I was born in Budapest. I was 52 years old at the time. Growing up suffused with tales like those in this book—a salad my father tossed with dollops of gallantry, mischief, charm, and kitsch—Budapest always seemed magically familiar. True, the Hungary of my father's bedtime stories had more in common with Oz than Austria. Its people were part Peter Pan, part Bilbo Baggins, and part Emperor Franz Jozsef. Teutonic with a twinkle and a wink. What child could resist a nation of such relentlessly playful adults?

When I remained awake after bedtime stories were done, I was often lulled to sleep by the undecipherable chatter of my parents' Hungarian friends, laughing and arguing in accents whose unique cadence provided the nurturing syncopation of my childhood.

And during the day there were the smells and the tastes of my mother's kitchen. I grew up nestled in among sautéing onions and peppers; stuffed in between apples, caraway seeds, and a roasting goose; propped on clouds of *galuska* in rivers of *paprikas* sauce; or rolled up into *palacsinta* and swaddled in apricot *lekvar*.

When I eventually visited Hungary in 1975 with my father, I was 24 and he was 69. It was his first trip back since the 1930s. He was crestfallen by how Budapest's vibrancy had been flattened, its laughter shushed into whispers. But to me it seemed alive and wonderfully evocative of the stories I had grown up with. We walked past Gundel's, the Café New York, Gerbaud— no less important emotional landmarks than Parliament and the National Museum.

We never returned to Budapest together. My father died a decade too soon to see the city's lurching renaissance, but in 2002 my wife and I went back with his younger brother Paul for a long autumn weekend, I felt instinctively that I had come home.

Paul had left in the early 1930s for Australia, where he buried himself in Anglophilia, embracing his new home. And yet, Paul told me in 2002 over dinner in a small Buda café (which he had scouted out in the impeccable Hungarian which he had spent decades denying he could remember at all) that he had dug out his 1935 Hungarian passport and reinstated his Hungarian citizenship. As a result, he said, my cousins—all native-born Australians—had become citizens as well.

I felt compelled to follow suit: My father had always seemed so much more Hungarian than Paul. Indeed, my father's Hungarian-ness was his defining characteristic. In some ways it was world-famous. In his public persona, he had been a George Washington Medal laureate of the American-Hungarian Foundation. Clandestinely, he had single-handedly provoked the 1956 Revolution. Or at least so the Communists claimed.

Starting out as a sports reporter for a sensationalist Budapest tabloid, my father became a stringer for British and American newspapers, stationed himself in Berlin, hung out on the fringes of the avant garde, and wrote sketches for German cabarets and witty commentary for Berlin newspapers. He became a war correspondent, sending dispatches for the pages of American and European newspapers from the front lines of wars we no longer remember. Like his brother, he left Europe young, in the early 1930s, several steps ahead of the Nazis, but unlike Paul my father brought his homeland with him. His accent, his hand-kissing charm, his love of the country of his birth; these were unmistakable.

He spent World War II in Washington, D.C., at a desk in Naval Intelligence, more or less inventing psychological warfare. After the war he found his way to Radio Free Europe. There, he conjured up an American intelligence agent, Col. Bell, who, together with a band of Hungarian stalwarts, took responsibility for every small disaster that befell Communist Hungary in the early 1950s. Bell seemed to be everywhere, responsible for a building collapse one week in Budapest, a fire in Debrecen the next. But, in truth. Col. Bell was nowhere at all, my father was just collating reports from Radio Free Europe's correspondents within Hungary who smuggled out news of local catastrophes so that Col. Bell and his band of virtual *agents provocateur* could lay claim to them. In this way, the United States appeared to have infiltrated Hungary already, providing a fictional but seductive infrastructure for the rebellion they hoped to foment. My father was assured that when the rebellion took root, genuine American troops would immediately back it up.

Once a week he broadcast a report of Col. Bell's most recent activities. Hungarians gathered around hidden radios and marveled at America's pervasive presence in their country. When the rebellion actually caught fire in 1956, however, America didn't follow through on its promises and the uprising was swiftly and tragically ground down under the treads of Russian tanks.

After the dust settled, the Communists issued a white paper in which they blamed Col. Bell for the whole thing.

Now Col. Bell's son was laying claim to a post-Communist Hungarian birthright. I had not realized, however, that to do so I would have to venture to the place where communism and capitalism meet: the deep foundation of petty bureaucracy on which both systems are built. I doubt that virtually any ripples were felt at the ministerial desks along the Danube in 1990, when department heads were ousted overnight but clerks and middle-managers merely rolled over in their sleep.

Inevitably, my citizenship application lay in their meticulous hands. After several months of silence, I was asked to provide supporting documentation. But I had already given them everything I had—including a copy of my father's birth certificate from Csurgo and my own from New York—and they acknowledged that the chain was proven beyond a reasonable doubt: he was born a Hungarian, I was his son. Still my father had chosen to marry a non-Hungarian (skeptical sidelong glance), and did so in Berlin (frown). I lacked a copy of his last Hungarian passport (deepening frown, wrinkling brow).

It turns out that there was, and still is I think, a law to the effect that a Hungarian loses his citizenship if he leaves the country for ten years without even a moment's layover back on Hungarian land. The post-Communist amnesty was available only to Hungarian citizens who had left under the Nazis or the Communists (after 1939 and before 1990). The Ministry needed to be convinced that my father had been in Hungary for at least one day during the ten years preceding 1939, or else he would have renounced his citizenship.

Would I be so good as to submit proof that Ladislas Farago had set foot in Hungary some time after 1929 (glower)?

This would not be easy. My father had lived with his parents, returning only sporadically once he became a foreign correspondent. His name did not appear independently in telephone or street directories, and proving that my grandparents or uncle had been there at the proper moment would do me no good at all (stern glare).

His byline appeared in Hungarian newspapers, but the Ministry frowned some more: those articles could well have been written outside Hungary; they did not constitute proof of presence. How about an affidavit from my uncle? Perhaps. They would have to see. They would let me know (officious cough). In the meanwhile, my application languished in its file folder and I heard nothing.

I consulted an experienced and well-connected immigration lawyer in Budapest. I paid the office a modest fee. I acquired the services of a talented young graduate law student who could translate for me, in the broadest sense of the word, at the Ministry. I was assured that with proper translation, the matter would be viewed sympathetically.

My translator and I returned to Buda, but the news was still equivocal. The ministry staff did indeed now wish they could be helpful. The frowns and doubts were replaced by shrugs, self-deprecatory bows, and apologies. If only we could come up with something that would demonstrate my father's physical presence in Hungary after 1929, they would be more than happy to help. Surely we must have something (ingratiating smile)?

We persevered. I asked my uncle for the affidavit. I started looking around for 90-year-old Hungarian eggheads who might recall my father from the Budapest nightlife he described in these pages. I hired a college student to research old newspapers to find articles by my father in which he reported first-hand about a Hungarian event (in vain).

None of these bore fruit. I vented to my small but sympathetic legal team. My father was an anticommunist stalwart. He believed himself to be a Hungarian to the day he died. He was so Hungarian that he had even written a book about it. This book—the very book you are holding in your hands—my father's only work of humor.

I sent a copy to my translator to demonstrate the depth of my father's Hungarian roots. How could the man who transcribed these stories, who captured so vividly the conmen and starlets of the demimonde, be denied his (and, by extension, my) Hungarian citizenship?

A week after sending the book to Budapest I got a call at home in New York. Jubilantly, my law student friend, who had by now graduated and was studying for the Bar, told me to pick up my copy. Exultantly, he ordered me to turn immediately to page 148 and read. I saw nothing special there. My father tells the story better, but my young friend was getting worked up about nothing more than the following tired but amusing old joke.

My father is sitting at his usual table at the Café New York. He has had a couple of cups of coffee and a ham roll. As he gets up to leave, the headwaiter, Lajos, presents him with a check for 47 pengoes, the equivalent of about $250. Shocked, and with only a few coins in his pocket, he asks Lajos how the check could possibly be that much. Lajos tells him that while today's bill amounts to only two pengoes; his arrears total 45. My father is irate:

"Don't be silly! Since when are you so hell-bent on collecting arrears?

"Since 1930, as far as you're concerned," Lajos responded.

And there we had it: My father. The Café New York. 1930.

That alignment, I was assured, would pay out the jackpot on the Ministry's slot machine. This, my young friend assured me, was a home run in the ballpark of bureaucracy.

I returned to Buda and to the Ministry, accompanied by my translator and gripping a photocopy of page 148 with Lajos' words highlighted in yellow marker. My file was found, the off-print added to it, and I swiftly received a document affirming my Hungarian citizenship. Not only that, but it was followed by my Hungarian birth certificate, my Hungarian marriage license, and the Hungarian birth certificate of my 17-year-old son, Max.

And so, on July 20, 2003, I suddenly had always been a Hungarian. In fact, through Max I was on my way to producing an entire Hungarian dynasty. And the whole thing grew out of that most enduringly Hungarian topsoil, the punchline of a charming, if somewhat stale, anecdote.

Like the story of my citizenship, the tales that follow derive from the Hungary of a century ago. A Hungary that perhaps never was, but that surely always will be. These are stories about the Hungary of my father's childhood and the Hungary of my middle age. They are distillations of the Hungary from before, during, and after the war – pick a war, any war. Above all else, they are the story of a country in which now, as always, the most important consequences can flow from whether or not one has paid one's tab at the Café New York.

JOHN FARAGO

The Importance of Being Hungarian

IT WAS AROUND 1530 A.D. THAT NICHOLAS COPERNICUS PUB-
lished his sensational *De revolutionibus orbium coelestium,* in
which he propounded that the earth, far from being the center
of the universe, was but a small planet revolving around the
sun.

That was some four hundred years ago but if the Hungarians
ever heard of it they chose to ignore the discovery. As far as
they are concerned, the sun continues to revolve around the
earth—and most important, it revolves around Hungary.

I became aware of this one morning in Budapest when I
heard our peasant maid tell my mother: "I can't understand,
madame, why people don't like the Jews. After all, wasn't our
Lord Jesus Christ himself a Jew before he became a Hungarian?"

There is a Hungarian saying, *"Az Isten is Janos,"* which in
free translation means that God himself is a Hungarian.

The most forceful negation of the Copernican theory was

1

expressed by my brother when he was given a globe for his seventh birthday. He categorically refused to accept the gift, crying: "I want a globe with only Hungary on it!"

This attitude, which Margaret Mead would undoubtedly diagnose as rampant ethnocentrism, was briskly promoted by Hungary's educational system, which viewed the world solely from the Hungarian angle. Thus Pope Sylvester, one of the greatest sages of the Church, was considered important in Hungarian history books only because he sent a royal crown to Hungary as a starter for a dynasty. Mohammed's historic significance was attested to us by the sole fact—if fact it was—that one of his concubines happened to be a Hungarian slave girl.

History as taught in Hungarian schools was an unbroken succession of Magyar triumphs. Not only were we assured that Attila the Scourge of God was, of course, a Hungarian but we also received a thinly veiled hint that Columbus, too, was of Magyar origin, only he found it more expedient in Spain to pose as a Genoese.

Thus I learned that, throughout her checkered history, Hungary was always victorious in all her wars, a claim I later found a little difficult to reconcile with the fact that most of the time she was occupied by foreigners—the Romans, the Turks, the Austrians and now the Russians. But such was the spell of Hungary that frequently the supposedly subjugated had the oppressor under their thumb.

The Turks in particular, who came to dinner and stayed for 173 years after a glorious Hungarian "victory" over them in 1526, enjoyed their sojourn hugely. There was little, if anything, of the usual tension between the forces of the occupying power and the occupied people. The Turks in Hungary soon did exactly as the Hungarians did. They are fondly remembered today mostly thanks to a gay philosopher named Gül Baba who transformed one of the spectacular hills that surround Budapest into a splendid botanical garden, covering its slopes with an exciting variety of roses the intoxicating fragrance of which still drifts across the Danube to lend the capital an unreal air of perfumed elegance.

In Hungarian textbooks, every discovery and invention ever made is claimed for a native son. The Gobi Desert in deepest East Asia, first explored presumably by Marco Polo, is assigned to a Hungarian explorer named Alexander Korosy. According to those same texts, the telephone was invented by a Hungarian engineer named Tivadar Puskas.

The jingoistic fire of such sanguine ethnocentrism is fanned by some truly great discoveries for which Hungarians have every proper right to claim and to get due credit. Thus the man who was really first to explore India's turbulent Northwest Frontier was Aurel Stein, a Hungarian archaeologist—a feat for which he received a knighthood from Queen Victoria. The doctor who made childbirth safe with his revolutionary discoveries in antiseptics was the Hungarian physician Ignaz Philip Semmelweiss. The physicist whose discoveries made the H-bomb possible was the Hungarian Edward L. Teller. America, of course, was discovered by Zsa Za Gabor, who, in turn, was discovered by an ebullient Hungarian editor, Sandor Incze, who also was the first to discover international beauty contests.

Hungary is a small country, about the size of Indiana, and there are only a relative handful of Hungarians at large in the world—some 10 million of them all told, of whom some 500,000 live in the United States. (Cleveland is said to be the second largest "Hungarian" city.)

For such a small country and such a handful of people, Hungary's contribution to all forms of human progress is truly phenomenal. When all ecological, demographical and characterological probings fail to provide a scientific explanation for it, this is usually attributed to an innate push, to the national proclivity for using one's elbows to get ahead and to the native ability of this remarkable race to fake a living where others less fortunate are forced to make one.

The widespread belief that the word "Hungarian" is merely a synonym for rogue or scoundrel or knave is reflected in innumerable quips paying left-handed tribute to them. One defines a Hungarian as a man who goes into a revolving door behind you but comes out ahead of you. Another claims that the recipe for Hungarian omelette begins: "Steal six eggs . . ." Still another asserts that during the halcyon days of Hollywood, when it was flooded with Hungarians from Vilma Banky to Paul Lukas and director Michael Curtiz, the studios displayed a sign reading: "It is not enough to be a Hungarian! You have to work, too!"

I once heard a prominent publisher say about one of his authors who happened to be Hungarian: "I'm darned if I know just what his motives are, except that I'm dead sure they are ulterior." Hungarians themselves repeat these quips with something akin to national pride, and add to the legend with remarks of their own in this same general category. Thus once a friend of mine explained to me the key to a successful career: "All you have to do," he said earnestly, "is to compromise your principles." When in the wake of their 1956 revolution, Hungarian Freedom Fighters flocked to this country, they were generously supported by all sorts of charitable organizations. This was acknowledged grudgingly by one of them, who told me: "So what! You'll see they'll get tired of it sooner or later and we'll have to go to work."

There are only two such quips Hungarians resent and, indeed, they are both rather malicious. According to one, a Hungarian is always willing to sell his country, his wife or his soul because he knows he'll never deliver it. The other, the most celebrated of them all, says: "If you have a Hungarian for a friend, you don't need any enemies."

Hungarians insist that such quips were coined by Austrians and Rumanians, who traditionally envied their charming and ebullient neighbors and who followed Hungarian triumphs in the world with jaundiced eyes. The quips do give a distorted picture of the Hungarian. They are not scoundrels by birthright. They are shrewd and ingenious. They are amazingly flexible and adaptable, eloquent and persuasive; their native charm is usually put to practical uses. Their national motto could be: "Don't work for things tomorrow that you can con today."

The true Hungarian appears to be out of this world and this makes some people think that Hungarians are people from another planet. The foremost exponent of this hypothesis is a distinguished Hungarian scholar, Dr. Theodor von Karman, one of the world's leading experts on space and proto-interplanetary travel.

According to von Karman, the Hungarians you are encountering are not Hungarians at all. They are Martians. One day, he claims, the powers on Mars resolved to conquer the Earth. The risks involved in such a gigantic enterprise were duly recognized and the Martian high command decided to reconnoiter the Earth first, then soften it up by infiltrators. A couple of hundred Martian fifth columnists were to be flown to Earth by flying saucers and the question was raised where they should land.

The United States was their logical goal, but the high command decided against America. They realized the Martians would have to be conditioned first and could enter the States only after they had learned to behave like earthlings. They sought a country where visitors from outer space would not be too conspicuous, where the people were used to peculiar creatures, if only because they themselves were a little odd.

Hungary seemed the ideal place, and the spearhead of the Martian force landed there. The newcomers mixed with the population and turned into earthlings, or rather into pseudo-earthlings. Some became scholars, others musicians or movie producers; still others took up writing or acting. Then, one by one, they infiltrated the United States. They found excellent jobs for themselves. They became prosperous, successful and influential. However, their real job was to undermine the morale of the American people and weaken their resistance for the decisive attack from Mars.

A chosen few had a special assignment. Their job was to coax the real earthlings into global suicide and to supply the means needed for their self-destruction. Thus the infiltrators became the moving spirits behind the development of the nuclear bombs.

When everything was ready for the showdown at last, a Martian expeditionary force appeared over the United States, all ready to land and conquer the Earth. They circled overhead in their huge flying saucers waiting for the signals they were supposed to get from their advance men. But no signals ever came!

What happened? "Simple," Dr. von Karman says. "Those pseudo-earthlings in the United States had adopted the characteristics of the Hungarians and double-crossed the Martians."

Dr. von Karman is fond of telling his hypothesis to anyone willing to listen, and I once heard him relate it to a group of senior officers from the U.S. Air Force. They received his tale with guffaws of laughter, but the learned scientist turned to me and said with a solemn mien: "You see? They think it's just a joke!"

No mundane worry can ever discourage a true Hungarian; his inborn optimism finds a silver lining even in the worst misfortune. Towards the end of the last world war, when everything was collapsing around them, the Germans would say woefully, "The situation is serious but not hopeless," while the Hungarians said "It is hopeless but not serious."

Their values are frequently cockeyed and, living as they usually do, mostly by their wits, for the pleasures of the moment rather than the rewards of tomorrow's maybe, they are satisfied with little, even if it may seem enormous to others. Shortly after their historic revolution, two penniless Freedom Fighters walked down Fifth Avenue bemoaning their life of hardship in exile. When they passed the Empire State Building, one of them said: "We wouldn't have any worries if we owned this preposterous building."

"Hell," said the other, "have you an idea of how much trouble you'd have just owning a building like this? The money you'd have to spend on just maintenance and what you would lose if a floor were vacant?"

"I'm not saying I'd keep it," the other returned. "I'd sell it fast."

"Fast?" the other remonstrated. "Do you know how difficult it is to find a buyer for such a monstrosity?"

"For twenty dollars?" the other concluded.

Others might find it difficult, if not impossible, to understand and appreciate Hungarians, just as I am sure we would find it not easy to understand a Martian suddenly appearing in our midst. But Hungarians understand and know themselves perfectly and appreciate one another—for theirs is a kind of secret society, like the ancient League of Assassins. Its rules and rites are known only to the initiated and its benefits accrue solely to them. Solidity may not be a Hungarian trait, but solidarity is, and it manifests itself in innumerable big and little things alien to all except Hungarians.

A Hungarian stranded abroad will always find support from another Hungarian, even if he is just as helpless as his compatriot—and a stranded Hungarian can be very stranded indeed. Hungarians are always great collaborators—they are constantly writing plays or novels together because as soon as one of them manages to sign a contract for a book or play he immediately wants his friend to share his good fortune and then, maybe, do the work for him.

Wherever they may be, Hungarians flock together, for they feel best and most at ease in each other's company. They can then indulge in their elaborate conversations, a strange form of *pourparler* in which everybody present talks effusively and simultaneously like trains running on parallel tracks, paying no heed to what the other fellow has to say.

This became pathetically evident to me during a trip to Moscow in 1937, the least likely place and time to make a study of Hungarians abroad. Like every capital city on earth, Moscow, too, had its Hungarian colony, inducing Ilya Ehrenburg to tell me: "It's a colony, alright, but we'd be glad to exchange it for a colony in Africa."

Moscow's expatriate Hungarians—mostly exiles from the short-lived Bela Kun regime of 1919—huddled together in a small room in a building on Kusnetsky Most that housed foreign intellectuals. I found them engaged in that simultaneous conversation, and when I succeeded in getting the gist of it I found they were not discussing Marx or the problems of agricultural collectives or dialectical materialism. They were talking about the Café New York, a famous landmark of Budapest where the country's intellectuals hang out; about the acacias in bloom in the Varosliget, Budapest's Central Park; and the relative qualities of *beef flanken* as prepared at Neiger's and at Gundel's, two of the city's best restaurants.

In London, a charming Hungarian once succeeded in seducing the telephone operator of a swank Mayfair hotel and gave her such a good time that the young lady, surfeited with gratitude, sat up in bed to say: "I say, honey, how come? I'm talking to blokes from all sorts of countries all the time, but only Hungarians are so nice to me. Now this is only February and the year is still young, but I have already had eleven Hungarians who invited me up to their rooms for a nightcap and then gladdened my life. Just what makes you Hungarians so nice?"

"Since you were so frank with me," the Hungarian replied, "I'll be truthful with you, darling." He kissed her hand gallantly and said: "Downstairs in the men's room, you see, there is a penciled note in Hungarian saying: 'Hungarians! The telephone operator going off duty at midnight makes love for free!' "

In their vibrant curiosity and with their restive imagination, Hungarians always have something up their sleeves. They are always deeply involved in something or other, either in some major research or minor mischief, in some grand illusion or petty larceny. Larceny, in fact, may always be on their minds but it is rarely in their hearts.

Thus Hungary produced some of the greatest men of our times but also many nebulous or nefarious characters. The discoverer of vitamin C—a Nobel Prize laureate professor named Albert von Szent-Gyorgyi—was Hungarian, but so was history's most dazzling con-man, Ignatius Trebitsch Lincoln, the only alien ever elected to membership in Britain's Parliament. Of the five scholars who pioneered in the military uses of atomic energy and developed the A-bomb, three—Szilard, Teller and Wigner—were Hungarians—and so were three of the five men arrested recently in Monaco for trying to break the bank of Monte Carlo with counterfeit chips and dice loaded so ingeniously that the smashing of the atom seemed mere child's play by comparison.

Bela Bartok, one of the greatest of all modern composers, was Hungarian, and so is Eva Bartok, the motion picture actress, whose eccentric antics burn holes into the tabloids.

Such wild diversification of authentic genius and false pretense, exceptional deeds and unadulterated corn, baffles the bystander, who regards all Hungarians with a mixture of awe, admiration and suspicion. To be sure, in Hungarians confusion has achieved its masterpiece. It is their good fortune or bad luck that their ears are forever ringing with the sound of a mysterious bell that nobody but Hungarians can hear. It summons them, as it did Duncan, either to heaven or to hell.

Molnar

THE DEW OF THE BUDAPEST DAWN WAS PAINTING THE WIN-
dow panes a dreary gray hue when a sleek *gummiradler*—a
hansom cab with pneumatic tires—rolled soundlessly to a stop
in front of a big patrician house. The coachman and his young
fare parted without a word, bidding farewell with friendly
little waves of their hands. The handsome young man—very
young indeed, for he was not yet twenty—was returning home
after a night on the town.

He unlocked the heavy door of the house, mounted two
flights on the gaslit stairway, then prepared himself for the
most perilous part of his stealthy homecoming—his surrepti-
tious entry into the apartment. He took off his shoes, untied his
flowing cravat, unfrocked himself to assure that the wings of
his jacket would not sweep off any of his mother's bric-a-brac
in the dark corridor through which he inched his way to his
bedroom.

The other members of the household—his physician-father,

11

his mother and the two maids—were high up in their forty winks, presumably oblivious to the son's return at this ungodly hour. He reached the bedroom without a hitch, closed the door quietly, then groped for a switch on the wall to turn on one of the luxuries of this affluent home (for this was the year 1897) —the electric light.

There at last, in the haven of his own room was this wanderer of the dawn, and there, too, sitting sphinx-like in a chair facing the door, was his mother, her eyes filled with sleep and reproach.

"What time is it, Feri?" she asked in a leaden voice. The young man, precise and polite as always, took a gold watch from a pocket of his waistcoat, looked at it and said:

"Four minutes past five, mamma."

"In the morning or in the afternoon?"

"In the morning, mamma."

"Well," she said, "do you consider this the proper time to come home, every night, night after night?"

"Oh, mamma," the young man said, determined to have it out once and for all, "you must not judge me by your own philistine standards. You still regard me as a child or maybe as a promising young lawyer who keeps regular hours, going to bed with the hens and rising with the rooster. But I am neither a child any more nor a lawyer as yet, and, for your information, it is not my intention of ever becoming one."

"Feri!" his mother said sharply.

"No, mamma," he said. "I am a writer! And writers may, as Shakespeare put it, disregard your conventional rules."

"No doubt," his mother said. "But tell me, Feri, does Mr. Shakespeare also go home to his father's house at four minutes past five o'clock every blasted morning?"

This delightful incident was related to me exactly fifty-four years after it happened by the erstwhile young man himself, Ferenc Molnar, the playwright, over luncheon in a New York restaurant called the Chateau Madrid. Molnar was fond of the place because it was discreet and quiet at noontime, when it served an excellent lunch at reasonable rates, while it was loud and garish, and rather expensive, at nights.

"This fascinating little dump has two faces," he used to say. "At lunchtime it is frequented by middle-aged ladies accompanied by young gentlemen, and at night by young ladies accompanied by middle-aged gentlemen."

The Chateau Madrid was on 58th Street in the heart of Manhattan, just west of Fifth Avenue, in the geographical center of Molnar's little world during his "years of exile" in New York. He lived in the stately old Plaza Hotel, rather frugally in a single back room on the eighth floor, in line with his principle that one should always stay in the cheapest room of the best hotel in town. His world in New York was confined to the Plaza and the block in which it stood. He rarely moved out of his enclave, in which he said he found everything he needed for both life and death—restaurants and bars, a dry cleaner and a doctor, a charming, statuesque young blonde for the few frivolous, although platonic, moments he still craved, everything at all, from a pharmacy to a funeral parlor.

His life in that single New York block seemed confined and drab, a far cry from his gregarious, magic years when he used to be the toast of Vienna and Paris, Europe's wit extraordinary and plenipotentiary, a fixture of the Côte d'Azur, a companion sought by royalty, and the lover of the Continent's most dazzling women. Yet Molnar knew how to infuse his seemingly austere life with grandeur and glamour, by decorating it with the facts and fancies of bygone days, and by surrounding himself with scintillating people, who continued to flock to him.

There in Room 835 of the Plaza was Greta Garbo, for instance, preparing coffee for Molnar on a tiny electric stove; and Gilbert Miller, the producer, forever plotting another Molnar play for the next Broadway season. There, too, were Ben

Hecht and Richard Rodgers, regaling him with their own memories, and Billy Rose, worshiping at his feet, with Leonard Lyons, the columnist, busily jotting down every anecdote.

I was his daily companion, a kind of paying guest for lunch at the Chateau Madrid, the last in a long succession of disciples whose sole function was to listen as he talked. In all his life, he needed an audience, for his stories maybe even more than for his plays. At this late stage, in the intimacy of the Chateau Madrid, he was content with an audience of one.

In my own youth in Budapest, I used to watch him in awe from a respectful distance as he presided majestically over round tables in the grand cafés, and envied those privileged to listen to his quips and tales. I became close to him only when it was almost too late. But he went out of his way to bring me up to date, retelling all his great stories and anecdotes with his old gusto and a last resurgence of his *joie de vivre*. Now, looking back on my luncheons with Molnar, I realize it was really a macabre experience, watching him relive his past by crowding all his memories into the little time he had left.

The day he told me the story of his furtive homecoming Molnar was reminiscing as usual, digging up the flippant memorabilia of his younger years. Now he was seventy-three years old, in what he called his "second awkward age." He was still as handsome as ever, the fresh, rosy complexion of his smooth and chubby face giving him a youthful appearance despite his snow-white hair. That hair! Next to his monocle it was his most celebrated trademark. It was not so lush and lustrous as it used to be, but still "adequate," as Molnar put it, for a man with one foot in the grave. He used a more forceful figure of speech that harked back to his days as a celebrated Don Juan, for women still dominated his thoughts and conversation, even if only in reminiscences.

During those days, he was seized by premonitions. References to death often sneaked parenthetically into his tales. He spoke of death with the bogus bravado of the inveterate cynic, now seriously, then mockingly; now defiantly, then hopefully. The fatal ailment that was to kill him a few months later was already working in him like slow poison. But he kept joking about death as he poked fun at everything, the most sacred as well as the most profane things.

In actual fact, Molnar relished life with passionate fervor and was morbidly afraid of the last curtain. Each day on our way back to the Plaza we passed a little funeral parlor on 58th Street the owner of which was frequently out on the street, observing the passers-by with an expectant look.

"A revolting fellow," Molnar would say. "Doesn't he remind you of the butcher in an abattoir appraising a poor little calf in which he sees merely a few pounds of veal for goulash?"

Like all the inhabitants of 58th Street, the undertaker was familiar with this immaculately groomed, white-haired, rosy-cheeked old gentleman. As soon as Molnar moved within reach of his voice, the undertaker would bow obsequiously and greet him with what sounded like a pleasant but somehow beckoning tone:

"Good afternoon, Miss-ter Moll-nar."

"No!" Molnar shot back at the top of his voice, for he dreaded even the nod of an undertaker.

He was shocked to his marrow whenever one or another of his contemporaries passed away. He was thus profoundly shaken when Ferenc Gondor, veteran editor of a Hungarian-language weekly and one of his oldest friends, suddenly died. Molnar knew that he was expected at Gondor's last rites at a fashionable funeral parlor on Madison Avenue, but he decided against going.

"I'm afraid," he quipped with a contrived smile, "they might keep me there."

He frequently spoke of that place on Madison Avenue, calling it a "despicable beauty parlor for the dead."

"Death," he once told me, "is depicted as the grim reaper with a scurvy head on an ugly skeleton, wrapped in a villainous black cape, brandishing that hideous scythe. Yet to me he is a charming and sociable fellow compared with the ghouls who smear rouge on the lips of corpses."

He had a storehouse of anecdotes for every occasion, including several about tribal funeral rites in the United States.

"I attended only a single funeral in New York," he told me, "in a so-called chapel somewhere on Amsterdam Avenue. It was the funeral of a dear friend who died of lung cancer, the poor soul, after a long illness that emaciated him.

"It was an impressive funeral. The chapel was filled with his relatives and friends. They were deep in mourning, because he was a much-loved man whose passing had shocked us. There they were, the mourners, haggard with eyes bloodshot from crying, with hollow cheeks in which there seemed to be not a drop of blood, looking like unattended corpses.

"There was but a single jaunty fellow in the whole confounded chapel. He looked chipper and fresh, his ruddy face radiating contentment and health, his lips drawn in an impish smile as if contemplating a risqué joke. He was on display in the open casket. He was the corpse."

Molnar wasn't able to relate his final anecdote because he never recovered consciousness after the operation that took him from us in 1952. It was left to Dr. Henry Lax, his friend and physician, to tell it. The playwright was already waiting on the operating table while seven doctors drifted in one by one to participate in the difficult operation. There was a round of introductions, none of the doctors paying any attention to Molnar, until he petulantly said:

"I'm the star of the show but nobody bothers to introduce me."

Five hours after his last quip Molnar was dead.

2

Hungarians live blithely suspended in a phantasmal space that is part Disneyland and part Donnybrook Fair. They entertain but a vague notion of the basic difference between what Browning called the plain, plump facts and their own gaseous fancy. In this never-never land, some of their dead go on living, like Sandor Petofi, for example, their greatest lyric poet and patriot. Petofi was killed in battle in 1849, yet he may still be seen wandering like a minstrel up and down Hungary, if you believe the folks who assure you they have just seen him, talked to him, dined and wined him, or put him up for the night.

Ferenc Molnar is a member in excellent standing of this exclusive club of Magyar ghosts. Hungarians talk of him as if he were still around, sipping his Dubonnet in the Park Chambers bar, talking a blue streak. This must suit Molnar on his cloud. He hated the idea of dying for the reason the French hate war—it interferes with conversation.

Molnar was born January 12, 1878, a perfect timing for him, because Hungary had just emerged from centuries of isolation and was moving with breathtaking speed into her orbit. By the time Molnar grew into young manhood, the nation was a glittering little satellite firmly established between heaven and earth.

He disliked talking of his life in cold statistics, and was autobiographical mostly in anecdotes. In Berlin in 1925, he was asked by Max Reinhardt to write a biographical sketch for a playbill. The note he eventually produced in some agony was confined to a bare listing of what he regarded as milestones in his life.

"I was born in Budapest in 1878," it read, "was a law student in Geneva in 1895, a journalist in Budapest in 1896, wrote a short story in 1897, a novel in 1900, had my first play

produced at home in 1902, abroad in 1908, became a war
correspondent in 1914, resumed writing in 1918, my hair
turned white in 1919, and now in 1925, I wish I were a law
student in Geneva again."

He became a legend already in his lifetime and now he is
beatified by his fellow Hungarians. To them he represents far
more than just a proud moment in their cultural history. Concealed behind their abstruse language (a branch of the Finno-
Ugric group now spoken, aside from Hungarians, only by two
Siberian tribes) they had greater poets and thinkers than Molnar. But Molnar became the symbol of their Golden Age, a
brief span as history goes, between their isolation prior to
1867 and their re-isolation after 1947.

Molnar was an eminently civilized and sophisticated man,
a polished cynic whose cynicism was so refined that it was frequently mistaken for philanthropy. He was a *bon vivant* in the
grand style, addicted to the most beautiful of women, the best
of foods, vintage wines, and yet he was a miser. He was so
penurious that few are those who can claim they ever succeeded in borrowing money from him. Once in Karlsbad, a
Bohemian spa he liked, an impoverished compatriot named
Kucsera spotted him on the promenade and accosted him for a
touch. Molnar was scandalized but, after some hesitation, he
fished out a twenty-crown bill, a pitifully small sum in Czecho-
slovak currency, and handed it to the petitioner.

Kucsera looked at the pittance with unbelieving eyes.

"What?" he exclaimed, "A Molnar giving twenty crowns?"

"No," the playwright said. "It isn't a Molnar giving it. It's
a Kucsera getting it."

When he moved to New York in 1940 and found that there
was but limited insurance (then only up to $5,000) to cover
bank deposits, he split up his fortune into $5,000 chunks and
deposited them in several different institutions.

He had the usual quota of relatives, of course, and many of

them looked to this fabulously successful scion of the family for financial aid. Once in the twenties, a large delegation of his relatives descended upon him in Vienna, where he was living in the cheapest room of the best hotel in town. Expecting an icy reception, they were surprised when Molnar greeted them in his friendliest manner and even suggested that they all pose for a family portrait.

When the print was delivered, he took it downstairs to the doorman of the hotel, instructing the man: "Keep this picture always at hand. Whenever you see any of the persons in the photo trying to get into the hotel, don't let him in."

He was just as niggardly in catering to his own needs, or so it seemed at least to people who visited him. In Budapest, even when he already enjoyed a supposedly enormous income, he lived in a modest three-room flat in a drab, lower-middle-class district. He was once visited there by a glamorous New York actress, paying homage after a long run in one of his plays on Broadway. She was scandalized to find Molnar living in that low-rent apartment.

Upon her return to New York, she spread the word about Molnar's apparent poverty and suggested that the books of the playwright's agent be audited because she suspected him of stealing Molnar's royalties. It needed a letter from Molnar himself to prevent her from starting a collection.

When the world-wide popularity of his plays made Budapest seem too limited for him, Molnar gave up his little flat on Zsigmond Street in Buda and moved into what he called his "new three-room apartment." It consisted of one room in a small hotel on St. Marguerite's Isle in Budapest, another in the Hotel Imperial in Vienna, and a third in the Hotel Negresco in Nice.

The only person he regularly supported was his daughter Martha, a self-effacing, shy woman who lived inconspicuously in the background of Molnar's spectacular life, refusing to cash in on her famous father's success or to leave Budapest for greener pastures. He sent her a monthly allowance until World War II (which found Hungary as usual on the wrong side) prevented him from doing so.

There is an anecdote relating to this, often told to illustrate Molnar's alleged stingy streak. The war was over and things were slowly returning to normal when Molnar supposedly bumped into a friend on 58th Street.

"Have you heard the bad news?" he asked the friend.

"What bad news?"

"One can again send money to Hungary."

Conscious of my role as Molnar's Boswell, I felt impelled to ask him about the authenticity of this anecdote. His face flushed and there was annoyance in his voice as he replied:

"No, it's spurious tattle. I am like a Christmas tree. Petty people keep hanging all sorts of cheap tinsel on me, for their own amusement. I used to be quite angry when I read in the columns wisecracks I've never made attributed to me. But what can I do? I have the reputation of having a quip for every occasion and those pygmies exploit me. I am no longer annoyed but I resent this one, on two grounds. For one thing, it really hurts me. For another, I don't think it is funny at all."

Despite his protestations, Molnar himself was quite willing to crack jokes about his finances, both as to his evident affluence and his apparent penury. When once he read about an enormous monthly stipend an American millionaire playboy was forced to pay his divorced wife, he burst into an angry denunciation of alimony, a system he regarded as far more despicable than blackmail or usury. He was proud that although he himself had divorced two wives, he never had to go on supporting them with those "obscene alms."

As a matter of fact, when he divorced his second wife, the celebrated Hungarian actress Sari Fedak, he was compelled by the terms of a property settlement to pay her a substantial balm. He was annoyed at first, but eventually he consoled himself. "Although we never kept a joint household," he said, "I used to have my dinner every night in Sari's apartment. The sum I was forced to pay her didn't amount to more than I would have had to pay if I had dined in restaurants all those years."

According to one of Molnar's stories, Emperor Francis Joseph of Austria-Hungary once visited Budapest and received the Minister of Culture and Education in private audience to inquire about arts and letters in Hungary.

"How are the painters doing?" His Majesty asked, and the Minister assured him they were doing fine.

"And the sculptors?"

"I am pleased to inform Your Majesty, their output is better than ever," the Minister said, then added: "And I am sure Your Majesty will be glad to hear that our writers are also in fine fettle, especially a promising young playwright . . ."

"I know," the Emperor interrupted him. "That fellow Molnar! He's making far too much money for his own good."

In actual fact, Molnar was not making the fortune everybody thought when his plays had their successful runs throughout the world and were bought by Hollywood for supposedly fabulous sums. Once when his wife, the actress Lilli Darvas, joined us for lunch at the Chateau Madrid to discuss a property Hollywood wanted, Molnar moodily recalled how badly the studios actually treated him.

"Everybody thinks," he said, "I've been getting God only knows what exorbitant sums from the movies. But do you know how much I received for *Liliom*, for example, and that after it became a hit on Broadway? *A total of seven hundred fifty dollars,* on which I had to pay two commissions, one to an agent in New York and another to one in Budapest."

The highest fee he ever received from Hollywood was paid by Paramount Pictures for his play *The Swan*, and even that amounted to only a little over thirty thousand dollars. He was parsimonious probably because he knew he was a notoriously bad businessman, completely dependent on his agents to make his deals for him. In a sense, too, he was ashamed to take money from Hollywood because he felt that any similarity between his original plays and what Hollywood made of them was purely coincidental. He called the fees from Hollywood "damages" for the use of his name on motion pictures allegedly based on his plays.

He suspected that his agents were somehow short-changing him because he saw them prospering on the sale of his plays. An inordinately shy man when it came to business negotiations, he needed his agents but regarded them as necessary evils and disliked them intensely. Once in Paris, a young woman accosted him in his favorite café, the Regence, introducing herself as the daughter of one of his agents. She was a pretty girl, exquisitely dressed, wearing a brand-new, expensive fur coat. When she left, Molnar turned to his companion.

"Did you see the gorgeous coat that girl was wearing?" he asked.

"Yes. What about it?"

"It was made of my skin."

3

Ferenc Molnar was a passionate Hungarian, and remained a starry-eyed devotee of Hungary even after he had left his native country and become a passionate American. He showed his devotion to the country of his birth by little gestures. His family name was Neumann but he changed it legally to Molnar in 1896 when it was *en vogue* to magyarize foreign family names on the occasion of Hungary's 1000th anniversary. He insisted that the peculiar Hungarian *aeiguille* always be affixed over the "á" in Molnar, and that his first name be left in its original as Ferenc, rather than translated into Francis or Franz or François, on foreign playbills.

He insisted, too, that the names of his characters be left in their original Hungarian no matter how much anguish the actors experienced in their efforts to pronounce them correctly. He always had the world premières of his plays in Budapest, even when foreign producers like Reinhardt and Belasco vied for the privilege of presenting them first.

"I'm afflicted with a strange disease," he told me, "Hungarian chauvinism. Being Hungarian is like a hole. The more you take away from it the bigger it becomes."

Molnar remained in Hungary as long as he could, even though life became well-nigh unbearable for him there on several grounds. He suffered from the rampant and malicious jealousies of his contemporaries, who viewed his success abroad with jaundiced eyes. He was nicknamed "Checkspeare," to indicate the importance of money in his creative art.

He left Hungary in the end but continued to write in Hungarian all his life. When after World War II a diplomat of the new Hungary called upon him in New York, inviting him officially to return in triumph to his native land, he was sorely tempted but refused in the end, telling the envoy:

"I am a Hungarian, yes! But now I am a citizen of the United States and enjoy my love affair with America. I found out in the past that one can never rekindle a broken liaison. At any rate, my dear friend, I never left Hungary. Hungary has left me."

As passionately as he loved her, just so passionately ashamed did he become when she went crazy with vulgar reactionary trends and introduced a vicious, official anti-Semitism that long preceded Hitler's in Germany. Even before that period, Molnar, as the most prominent Jew in Hungary, had been singled out for ambiguous treatment—recognition to his face, malicious discrimination behind his back. He was never elected a member of the Royal Academy and was never produced in the National Theatre.

Molnar was a confirmed monarchist, not on any political grounds, but because he enjoyed the posh tranquillity of the days when Hungary still had a king. Molnar worked his nostalgia for the defunct monarchy into a bitter-sweet comedy, *The Swan,* in which the head of a dethroned dynasty hopes to revive the past glory of his house by marrying off his daughter to a reigning prince. A corny, romantic plot, it was the closest to a political point of view Molnar ever expressed in his writings.

Several theatres in Budapest competed for the play but Molnar hoped it would be produced by the National, the ultimate accolade a Hungarian playwright could receive. Knowing how anxious he was to see *The Swan* on the National's stage (he actually wrote it for its lovely leading lady, Gizi Bajor), his friends pulled strings behind his back. In the end, Sandor Hevesi, the National's director-general, put in a bid. Molnar was overjoyed to give him the play.

As soon as it became known that *The Swan* would be produced by the National, a rabid anti-Semitic gang called "Awakening Hungarians" threatened to make trouble. The Minister of Education, who had the last word in the management of the nation's first theatre, got cold feet and instructed Hevesi to cancel the deal.

Hevesi, himself a Jew, was deeply embarrassed by this turn of events, but lacked the backbone to create an issue over the ban or to resign in protest. Molnar dismissed him with contempt. "Poor Hevesi," he said, "he is like the colored doorman in a southern hotel in the United States whose job is to keep the Negroes out." From then on, he referred to Hevesi only as "that colored doorman."

Shortly after the cancellation, Molnar bumped into the Minister of Education at a party in the newspapermen's club, the Otthon. His Excellency apologized to him and tried to make up for the humiliation with noisome flattery. Molnar found the hypocrisy repugnant.

"You are, sir," he told the Minister, "like the man who takes a little fish from a creek, holds it in his palm and strokes it with tender care, yet closes his eyes to the fact that the poor little thing, kept out of its element, is bound to die in those caressing hands." Then, telling the baffled Minister, "I don't think I care to remain under the same roof with Your Excellency," Molnar turned around and marched out of the party in the bravest demonstration against Hungary's reactionary regime.

Budapest was thrilled but startled by Molnar's bold act because he was not considered a particularly bold or brave man. If anything, he was supposed to be a coward, a reputation he himself liked to encourage. During the restive revolutionary days after World War I, Molnar refused invitations to parties, candidly conceding that he did not dare to go out on the streets after dark. Once a sculptor friend of his named Dezso Lanyi, an enormously powerful man, volunteered to act as his bodyguard, but Molnar turned him down: "You are so big and strong," he told Lanyi, "aren't you afraid that *you* might kill someone?"

When he could not evade an invitation, he would hire a hansom for the trip, have its top put up to screen the rear, then seat himself up front with the coachman, talking all the time to the empty back seats to give the impression that he was not alone. He loved those horse-drawn hacks and was not at all enchanted when progress replaced them with motorized cabs. When he bought an automobile, he had a horn installed in the back seat and honked it vigorously at the slightest provocation. He so confused his chauffeur that the poor man drove into another car and that soured Molnar on private automobiles for the rest of his life.

He was especially afraid of fires and lived with the premonition that one day he would perish in a conflagration in his own home. One of the reasons he had kept his little apartment on Zsigmond Street in Buda was that it happened to be just across from a hook and ladder company. Once he entertained the Lord Mayor of Budapest in his little flat and asked His Honor to say a good word on his behalf to the firemen downstairs. His Honor stepped out on the balcony, summoned the firemen to assemble in front of the fire house, then instructed them to take particularly good care of the house in which the playwright lived.

Much later in New York, a friend asked Molnar to spend a weekend in his home at Woodstock, New York. It was a stifling hot summer and Molnar toyed with the idea of getting some relief by spending a few days in the country. But he had certain reservations:

"That country home of yours," he asked the friend, "is it a stone house?"

"No," the friend said, "it's a frame cottage."

Molnar's face darkened. He recalled the headlines announcing how whole families frequently perished in flash fires consuming frame cottages. He still hoped to go, so he asked the friend:

"Do you keep fire extinguishers and other fire-fighting equipment at hand, in case of fire?"

"No," the friend said, "but I'd be delighted to buy those things if that would put your mind at ease and make you come."

The friend bought fire extinguishers for every room, plus sand, buckets and axes. The day before Molnar's scheduled arrival, the friend traveled to Woodstock with the equipment. Approaching the hill on which his house stood, he saw ominous black smoke curdle skyward in the distance. His house was a heap of charred ruins when he reached it. When he told the playwright about the tragedy, he commented:

"Strange, this premonition of yours, Feri. How could you know what'd happen?"

"Oh," Molnar said, "I'm just a pessimist, and unfortunately, in this world of ours, the pessimists always turn out to be right."

Molnar could be quite courageous on occasions but only when he faced danger without being aware of it. Once during his halcyon days in Budapest, he was invited by Andor Miklos, publisher of *Az Est*, the country's biggest daily, to spend a weekend on his estate at Szentendre on the Danube, about an hour's ride from the capital. When Molnar arrived, he found a most embarrassing situation awaiting him. Among the other guests were a famous young actress and Count Nicholas Szechenyi, a celebrated *boulevardier*. That would not have been too bad by itself, had not the actress, a bewitching woman married to a famous actor, been the Count's mistress while also involved in a clandestine liaison with Molnar. Her husband could not help knowing about her romantic entanglement with Szechenyi, for it was the talk of the town. But he knew nothing of her affair with Molnar. On the other hand, the Count knew that she was betraying him with the playwright.

If this sounds rather complicated, it is because such *amourettes* were frequently very involved, indeed, in Budapest. Brought under the same roof with his secret mistress as well as his rival, Molnar was not amused at all. He put up a brave front because he did not cherish the idea of fighting a duel with Szechenyi, a well-known swordsman, and so the weekend passed without an open clash.

At breakfast on Sunday, the actress announced she would have to return to Budapest in the afternoon because she was scheduled to appear in a play that night. Molnar expected the

Count to accompany her but was startled when Szechenyi told
their host: "My car will take madame to town, but if you don't
mind, I'd like to linger on for one more night at this delightful
place."

Molnar dreaded the thought of remaining behind, alone with
Szechenyi, who both bored and alarmed him. He told Miklos
that he, too, would have to return to the city.

"You can ride with madame in my car," the Count suggested
in his most endearing tone.

The playwright was flabbergasted. He suspected a fiendish
ruse, but he could not very well refuse, so he rode to Budapest
with the actress in Szechenyi's Rolls-Royce. As soon as
Szechenyi returned to his *palais* in town, Molnar paid a formal
call on him to assuage his curiosity.

"Frankly," he said, "I couldn't sleep a wink last night, trying
to figure out why you permitted me to ride home alone with
our little friend. I made up my mind to find out your reason.
Tell me, my dear Count, just what in the world made you so
recklessly generous?"

Szechenyi flashed his best smile, as he said: "I'm of course
not obliged to tell you my reasons if, indeed, I had any. However, I'll let you in on a little secret. Sunday morning I received an urgent call from my secretary in Budapest, warning me that the husband of our dear actress found out she
would be returning to the city that same afternoon. Assuming
that I would accompany her, he decided to ambush us on the
road and shoot me down. I regret that his plans went awry, for
reasons I do not presume to know, but maybe you could use
this rather gruesome episode in one of your future plays."

4

In Budapest, Molnar became the founder of a rather prag-
matic literary school, when a sophomoric group of young play-

wrights hoped to coast to fame and fortune on his coattails. They copied his plots and style, patterned whimsical little efforts after his masterpieces, and their lives after his life. He ruled over them indolently, but with an iron hand. First in the Café Central, a staid literary coffeehouse the windows of which opened on an ancient Franciscan church, and then in the Café New York, Molnar held sway. He lectured incessantly to his disciples about anything that happened to pop into his mind, discoursing with insurpassable, insolent wit in preposterously arbitrary terms, tolerating neither contradictions nor interruptions.

Those were his happiest days, and he told me he had enjoyed them more than any other period in his life. When he was still the sage of the Café Central, shortly after World War I, he was invited to visit New York, where *Liliom* was a big hit starring Eva Le Gallienne and Joseph Schildkraut. Molnar refused to go. "I dread the trip," he told his New York agent, who had personally conveyed the invitation to him.

"But why?" the agent protested. "You'll travel in perfect luxury, first on the Orient Express, then on the finest ocean liner, which has the comforts of a first rate hotel."

"Yes," Molnar said, "but what about the trip from this coffeehouse to the railroad station?"

Molnar's way of life was as sophisticated as his plots. He rose late in the afternoon, dressed with great care, drove to the Café New York in a cab and had breakfast at eight o'clock in the evening. Around eleven, he had a date, usually with a popular actress just coming off the stage, and took her to an elegant restaurant where she had supper and he lunch. He escorted her home, then returned to the New York, where around seven in the morning he had dinner, going home and to bed at eight o'clock.

He worked at the New York during the wee hours, writing his plays and novels in pearly longhand at a little marble-topped table on a second-floor balcony, oblivious to the noise around him and even getting inspiration from the café's military brass band. His habit of working in coffeehouses scandalized his mother. In 1909, when *Liliom* was first produced in Budapest and flopped so badly that most of the audience fled from the theatre before the final curtain, she summoned Molnar home and told him:

"Now you can see for yourself, Feri, what happens when one writes plays in a coffeehouse."

Only once was an attempt made to domesticate him, and then but briefly by his first wife, the daughter of Budapest's dean of editors and a brilliant author in her own right, Margit Veszi by name. She frowned on Molnar's nomadic gypsy life and insisted that he settle down to work at home. She gave him the airiest, lightest, most cheerful room in their apartment for his study, furnished it with exquisite care, then told Molnar: "Now work!"

"The study had an enormous antique mahogany desk with a genuine Louis XV inkwell," Molnar recalled, "soft armchairs and a cozy sofa, everything except a brass band. And without that I could not work."

He solved the problem by divorcing his wife, giving her custody of the desk and the inkwell, while he himself returned to the New York. It was there, to the accompaniment of brassy military marches, that he wrote his most tender and sensitive novel, *The Paul Street Boys,* as well as *Liliom.*

I was once told that Molnar had patterned *Liliom* after himself and I asked him whether it was true.

"I really don't know," he said. "Not consciously, I'm sure. But it is entirely possible that I did write into *Liliom* some of my own sentiments and foibles, my attitudes to women, for instance, and especially my love of the underdog. *Liliom* came out a selfish, priggish charlatan and a cynic, although I did not see him like that when he first occurred to me. I visualized him rather as a massive, roughly hewn figure like a Rodin statue—sharp and unfinished at the edges, but solid in his core, a tormented soul torn between his callousness and his remorse."

The most touching scene in the play is when Liliom, going on parole from heaven to perform a single redeeming deed by visiting the home he had wrecked, steals a star as his gift for the daughter he has never seen. It is an act of whimsical larceny, lending the play its warmest touch. But it was not Molnar's idea at all. It was suggested to him by a stagehand during a rehearsal, and Molnar wrote it in for its obvious theatrical effect.

Molnar had the reputation of being a monumental egotist in the mold of Dorian Gray. While deep in his soul he resented the dubious distinction, he rarely tried to deny or discourage it. He was, indeed, highly opinionated and rampant with bias, harsh in his judgment of others, and rather vindictive. When the great Hungarian cartoonist Emery Kelen drew what Molnar considered an unflattering caricature of him, the playwright broke with Kelen and refused to talk to him for a whole decade. He was probably the century's greatest raconteur, but his wit had vicious barbs and he did not care whom it might hurt. He enjoyed friendships and had many great and lasting ones, but he never hesitated to break them on the flimsiest, most esoteric grounds. He thus broke with one of his dearest friends, the poet Jeno Heltai, because once he dreamt he was being hanged in public and spotted Heltai grinning in the crowd.

He was fond of spinning characters apparently out of thin air, an *enfant terrible* named "Józsi," for instance and a mythical figure of furtive malice he called the "Wicked Man." He conceded that he had patterned "Józsi" after himself. He himself used to be an insufferable brat, playing such violent jokes that one of them fractured his grandmother, literally fractured her, because the old lady broke her leg by falling into one of her grandson's traps. However, he steadfastly refused to acknowledge that the "Wicked Man" had any relationship with him. Molnar had him follow for hours a nurse carrying a babe in her arms in the hope that maybe she might drop the infant. Around Christmas, the "Wicked Man" amused himself by throwing lighted matches into mailboxes to destroy all those contemptible greetings of good cheer. His favorite pastime was to visit the city's most exclusive cemetery, walk up to a palatial mausoleum in which the town's richest man reposed in his eternal slumber, and say out loud: "It's now seven o'clock in the evening, sir, and I'm going to Gundel's for dinner, but you sir, are going to stay right here."

Molnar refused to see any premeditated malice in his own barbs and rather regarded himself as an accomplished practical joker. One of his victims was Victor Jacobi, the sensitive young composer, who always put all his soul into his art. Once on his nocturnal wanderings Molnar happened to pass Jacobi's ground floor apartment and through the open window heard Jacobi writing a number for his next operetta. The composer appeared to be deeply impressed with the tune, for he played it again and again on the piano and hummed it as he played, until Molnar, who had planted himself under the window, learned it by heart.

A few days later, Jacobi bumped into Molnar in a café. Hardly had he made himself comfortable at Molnar's table when the playwright began to hum the lovely tune. Jacobi paled: "That tune, Feri! What was it you just hummed?"

"Oh, that," Molnar said nonchalantly. "It's a waltz from a new French musical. It's very popular in Paris just now."

Jacobi trembled. "Who wrote it?"

"I really don't know," Molnar said lightly. "I think Audran or Lecocq, or maybe Planquette. No, no! Now I remember.

It's by Hervé. I couldn't help remembering it since I was in Paris last month."

But when he looked up, he saw that Jacobi was close to collapsing, tears streaming from his eyes. He realized he had carried the joke too far and told the composer the truth.

Gilbert Miller once cabled Molnar from New York that he would be coming to Europe and he hoped to see him, preferably in Vienna, to discuss an urgent matter of mutual interest. Molnar was planning to go to the Riviera, but stayed in Vienna instead to await Miller's arrival. While he waited, he received daily cables from the producer, from the boat, then from London and Paris and Zurich, signifying his approach. Then silence! Molnar found out from the newspapers that Miller had arrived in Vienna. But he didn't hear from the producer himself.

At last, Miller called—from Salzburg.

"My dear Feri," he pleaded, "I was so busy in Vienna that I simply didn't have time to get in touch with you. However, I must see you. I'm here in Salzburg, in Max Reinhardt's castle as his guest. Please do me the favor and join me here; it's imperative we meet."

Molnar was annoyed but he decided to go. Miller received him jubilantly.

"Reinhardt is going out of his way to entertain me," he told him. "He's giving a banquet in my honor tonight and the guests include Austria's most important men. The Chancellor himself will be there, as well as the Cardinal-Archbishop and the commanding general of the military district. I'm so pleased and excited! I hope you can stay!"

Molnar was fuming but he already had the perfect plot to pay back the humiliation. A few hours later, he went to Miller and told him:

"I really don't know, dear Gilbert, whether I should tell you this, because it's so embarrassing, but after all . . ."

"What is it?" Miller asked.

"No," Molnar said, as if changing his mind, "I don't want to be a kill-joy and certainly don't want to come between you and Reinhardt."

"Ferenc, for God's sake," Miller insisted, "you must tell me, no matter what!"

"Well, if you insist. But you must promise not to get angry with Reinhardt. I'm sure he meant well."

"What is it?" Miller asked again, now darkly and pleadingly.

"The banquet tonight . . ." Molnar said.

"What about the banquet?"

"The distinguished guests Reinhardt assembled for you . . ."

"What about them?"

"Well," Molnar said slowly, "they are not, how shall I say, what they're cracked up to be. The Chancellor, the Cardinal-Archbishop, the commanding general—they are . . . No, I don't think I ought to disillusion you."

"Ferenc, you must tell me the truth. What about them?"

"They are all extras and minor actors from Reinhardt's theatre in Vienna. He must want something very badly from you, because he imported them for the dinner to butter you up."

"You're joking."

"Would I dare in a matter like this? I can't understand Reinhardt. I thought he was a man of dignity."

"I am outraged," Miller said. "I don't know what to do."

"If you'll allow me to give you some advice," Molnar said solicitously. "I would do nothing if I were you, not just yet. Let Reinhardt have his fun! After all, now that you know his secret, you hold the joker."

"What do you suggest?"

"Go through with the banquet. Let the Chancellor and the Cardinal-Archbishop deliver their blasted speeches honoring you. Let the commanding general propose the toast to you. But then, when your turn comes . . ."

"Yes?" Miller asked eagerly.

"I would get up and tell them off, expose them, unveil them, and walk out on them, showing them that you cannot be made a fool of, not even in a special production by the esteemed Max Reinhardt."

And so it came to pass. But when the scandal broke and Miller walked out in apoplectic anger on the real Chancellor of Austria, the genuine Cardinal-Archbishop of Salzburg, and all the other distinguished guests around Max Reinhardt's festive table, Molnar was in a train on his way back to Vienna, sleeping soundly in his first-class compartment like an innocent babe, smiling in his dreams.

Maybe it was the surmised proximity of death that mellowed him, but I never saw Molnar in a vindictive mood or heard him indulge in his celebrated malicious humor. As a matter of fact, the Molnar I knew so intimately during the last year of his life was a humble man, considerate of others, even if not to the extent of picking up their tabs when lunching with him at the Chateau Madrid. According to legend, the first two English words he learned upon his arrival in New York were: "Separate checks." Even when he had his wife, Lilli Darvas, for lunch—they were living separately although not legally separated—he would preface the meal with them.

His humility was evident to me when he once spoke of George S. Kaufman, the playwright, and praised him in exaggerated terms, then added ruefully:

"Unfortunately, I never had the pleasure of meeting him. Apparently, he dislikes me, maybe even loathes me, I don't know why, because I've never done anything to hurt him and yet he hurt me so savagely in that frightful spoof *Bravo*."

Bravo was a minor opus Kaufman wrote in 1948, in which he satirized a Continental playwright obviously patterned after Molnar. I did not know Molnar felt so insulted by it, because, as a matter of fact, his wife, Lilli Darvas, played one of the parts in the feeble Max Gordon production.

It so happened that I was then seeing Gordon with some regularity and heard him talk about Molnar in a similarly nostalgic tone. "I'd love to meet him, and so would George," Max said, "but we are afraid he must be awfully mad with us because of *Bravo*."

So now I hastened to reassure Molnar. "They aren't at all what you think they are. As a matter of fact," I said, "Gordon told me only a day or two ago that they'd like to meet you but they're afraid to make the first move because they fear you're angry with them."

"I'd be delighted to see them," Molnar said with evident relief, "if you could arrange a luncheon."

Gordon suggested that we meet the following Friday at his sister's home, where a sumptuous Hungarian lunch was served every Friday to a select coterie of guests Gordon wanted to treat to that diabolic food. Molnar was eager to accept the invitation but his doctor turned thumbs down on it, and so I arranged for a luncheon at the Chateau Madrid.

I looked forward to the meal with breathless expectation, thinking of the opportunity of sitting in on the clash of two of the age's greatest wits. It turned out to be a dismal affair. Kaufman came, accompanied by Gordon, and everything was sweetness and light, Molnar apparently enchanting Broadway's celebrated curmudgeon with his effusive charm and hospitality. As a result, there was no war of wits, none of the bright, sparkling conversation I expected. Here met two exceptional men, both infatuated with the sound of their voices and overflowing with things they wanted to get off their chests. Throughout the meal, Molnar and Kaufman both talked incessantly and simultaneously, not to each other—they just talked. There was no exchange of ideas or any high-spirited sparring, no anecdotes flying to and fro, no witticism to be remembered, just plain talk, and it was difficult to follow because this was a frantic two-ring circus with a star performing in each ring.

Only once during the lunch was there an exchange between the two, and it developed into an acrimonious argument. Molnar was talking about the Broadway stage, bemoaning the fact that its fate depended on a handful of aloof men—the drama critics—who could make or break a play. He warmed up to the subject and talked in strong words against the critics, provoking George Kaufman to rush to their defense. Probably Molnar did not know that Kaufman himself had once been a drama critic and thus had a vested relationship with the clan. It is possible, though, that Kaufman did not give a hoot about the critics and secretly shared Molnar's annoyance with them, but defended them merely to be contrary. Whatever it was, the luncheon ended on a sour note, Molnar showing his annoyance by telling the waiter:

"Separate checks."

 *Playwrights*

A SOUFFLÉ IS DEFINED BY WEBSTER AS A LIGHT AND FLUFFY dish that is made frothy by beating and is precariously fixed in that condition by heat. A few decades ago, the term was applied by the New York drama critics to one of Hungary's most popular exports—situation comedies.

Patterned after Molnar's lighter plays, these fragile little dramatic concoctions were entertaining enough and did a lot of good for tired businessmen, suburban matrons and other theatregoers not keyed to the more earnest efforts of Clifford Odets. But the critics refused to take them seriously and usually souffléed them to death.

They generally had a second life, though—far more glittering than the first. They were grabbed up by Hollywood and made into charming little celluloid comedies by the expert hands of Ernst Lubitsch and Hungarian directors like Alexander Korda, George Cukor and Mike Curtiz.

Thanks to Hollywood, the soufflés became enormously lucrative and their production developed into one of Budapest's major industries. In every literary café along the Ring you could see sleepy-eyed, unshaven, pale young men whispering in secretive huddles or hunched over little marble-top tables with pen in hand. They were either plotting a soufflé or actually writing one.

Behind much of this was a strange entrepreneur, an individual as remote and mysterious as the Old Man of the Mountain. He was a lawyer named Ladislas Rakosi, a tall, severely groomed, pedantic-looking man, who had given up his legal practice to become a playbroker and before long was operating a gilded mousetrap to which Broadway and Hollywood producers beat a path. He was the kind of literary agent who is more important, and usually more prosperous, than the writers he represents.

It isn't quite correct to call him an agent, either, because he was not just a conveyor belt between author and producer and he was most certainly not a "ten percenter." He was a capitalist, like the operator of a steel factory or the proprietor of a chain of elegant brothels. Rakosi operated a soufflé factory, baking them as fast as possible, then dumping them on the little theatres of the world, especially on Broadway and Hollywood.

He bought the plays outright from their authors and made a fortune for himself from the huge fees Hollywood eventually paid. Yet he was widely regarded as a genuine philanthropist, a benefactor of the dramatic art of Hungary. Without his fees most of the sleepy-eyed young writers would have had to choose between starving to death or—even worse—selling haberdashery.

Dr. Rakosi's huge play factory produced a few authentic talents of enduring quality, including the Three Laszlos— Laszlo Fodor, Laszlo Bus-Fekete and Laszlo Vadnai—but most of his young writers had but a brief bloom. They concocted a play or two, then decided haberdashery was easier. Even so, Rakosi's zeal and business acumen kept the factory humming. During those days, when you inquired of any sleepy-eyed young Hungarian writer what he was working on, he would invariably say: "I'm writing a play for Hollywood." And he would be telling the truth most of the time.

I myself could not escape the fate that thus befell the majority of my counterparts, and before long I was on the payroll of the Rakosi Soufflé Factory, writing a play for Hollywood.

It all began on one of those rainy afternoons that later inspired *Gloomy Sunday,* the celebrated Hungarian song that attained a macabre global popularity and was blamed for more suicides than blighted love or embezzlement. I did not have a red cent to my name and no apparent prospect of earning one within the foreseeable future. I sat in the Café New York, staring dejectedly into a glass of black coffee, called *fekete,* contemplating my most immediate problem, which was how to pay for the *fekete.*

The huge coffeehouse was almost empty. Nobody among those present appeared an even remotely promising prospect for a touch. Most of my fellow guests were hollow-eyed, unshaven young men, staring dejectedly into tall glasses of black coffee.

I had a brief spell of hope when Zoltan Baroti came into the café and sat down at my table. Zoltan was gainfully employed as a reporter on an afternoon newspaper and sometimes had some money around the first and the fifteenth. Unhappily this was the fourteenth. He ordered a glass of black coffee, then the two of us just sat there, staring into our respective glasses.

Our introspective contemplation was broken by the expressive arrival of Dr. Rakosi. He sauntered into the café and surveyed the dismal scene with the bored glance of an inspector from the Welfare Department.

Zoltan kicked me under the table. "There is Rakosi," he said.

"So what?" I answered lethargically. "You know he is the town's most difficult touch."

"Yes," Zoltan said, "but perhaps we could sell him a play."

"What play?"

"What difference does it make?" he asked impatiently, got up, made straight for Rakosi and engaged him in what seemed to be a spirited conversation. The next thing I saw was Zoltan piloting Rakosi to our table.

"I have told Dr. Rakosi about the play we are doing," Zoltan told me, "and he is, of course, interested."

"Of course," I said.

"The plot idea Zoltan has just sketched briefly has some possibilities," Rakosi said, "and the fact that the play has only three characters and one set makes it, of course, a promising property."

"Of course," I said.

"Now tell me more about the plot," he turned to Zoltan. "What happens after the Grand Duke loses his kingdom at baccarat?"

"Ah," Zoltan said mysteriously, "that is our little secret, sir."

"I'm not trying to rush you, boys," Rakosi said. "When you have the time and are ready, come and see me in my office. I'll see what I can do for you." He got up to leave. Zoltan mounted the charge.

"We're not trying to put you off, Dr. Rakosi," he said casually. "We could even seal the agreement now with a bit of an advance."

"An advance, of course," Rakosi said mechanically.

"Of course," I said.

Rakosi reached into his pocket and gave Zoltan a ten-pengoe bill. Then he left to make the rounds, handing out ten-pengoe bills at various tables.

When Rakosi was out of hearing, I said to Zoltan: "I didn't know we were writing a play."

"We needed the money, didn't we?" he shot back. "And Rakosi was our only chance."

"Of course," I said.

"Maybe it wouldn't be such a bad idea if we did write a play after all. Everybody else is doing it."

"Not such a bad idea at that," I said.

"Well," Zoltan asked, "have you got an idea for a plot?"

"A plot?" I said. "I thought you just gave Rakosi a plot. He seemed to like it, too."

"I improvised," Zoltan explained. "Do you think I could've asked him for the dough without offering anything?"

"Well, how about your improvisation?"

"Oh, that?" Zoltan reflected pensively. "We can't use that. I told him the plot of *The Merry Widow,* of course."

"Of course," I said, and ordered a blue plate of cold cuts because, thanks to Dr. Rakosi, I could eat again.

The news of our deal with Rakosi spread like wildfire from the Café New York to the Club Parakeet, to the chorus line of the Parisian Grill and to an establishment called Maison Frieda, an elegant little mansion where a night on the town usually ended in the company of scantily dressed young ladies who were always ready to retire on a moment's notice to one of the palazzo's elaborately mirrored or oak-paneled bedchambers.

A deal with Rakosi was more potent than a credit card is today. It opened up endless financial vistas with headwaiters, starlets and Madame Frieda. I urged Zoltan that we postpone the celebrations until after we had the plot worked out. He was inclined to agree, but we had no choice. We simply could not evade the obligations of our new noblesse and disappoint the headwaiters, starlets and Madame Frieda.

We woke up the next day in adjoining bedchambers at Maison Frieda with a malaise mixed of hangover and remorse. It was three o'clock in the afternoon.

An hour later we confronted Rakosi in his office. We did not have even a hint of an idea. Zoltan approached our ordeal with fatalism and equanimity. He felt he had done his part by getting us that far. From then on, he expected me to carry the ball. So when we sat down in Rakosi's office he solemnly told the lawyer that I was the one who would outline the plot.

I looked around the room desperately searching an idea for a starter from the pictures on the wall or the bric-a-brac on Rakosi's desk. They had no message for me. My mind was completely blank. I was beginning to fear the worst when suddenly I heard myself begin to talk as if I were a jukebox that has just been fed a coin.

"The curtain rises," I heard myself say, "on an intimate but elegant party in the town house of Grand Duke Fedor. The guests are dancing a gay gavotte to a tune by Couperin, when . . ."

"Wait a moment," Rakosi interjected. "I thought there were only three characters in the play?"

"Of course," I said hastily. "The dancing is off stage, what else? It is merely indicated by the soft gavotte music floating in when the Duke enters through the center door. He is accompanied by Nina, the great soprano. It is her triumph in *La Traviata* that the Duke's party is celebrating. Also present at the gala affair is Alfred, the tenor who is Nina's husband. This creates a rather embarrassing situation because Nina is also the Duke's mistress. The Duchess is away at her country estate—or at least that is what the Duke thinks. Suddenly the music stops. You can hear startled ohs and ahs from off-stage. Then the center door opens and Alfred enters, catching the

Duke with Nina in his arms. Peremptorily sending Nina away, Alfred confronts the Duke. His first thought is to challenge him to a duel, but suddenly he gets a far more brilliant idea—an inspiration caused by the unexpected entrance of the Duchess Appollonia . . ."

"Wait a moment," Rakosi said. "Duke, Duchess, Alfred, Nina—that makes four. Now let's get this straight, boys, is this a three-character play or isn't it?"

"Of course it is," I said. "The actress who plays Nina also plays Appollonia. A tour de force! A simply terrific challenge to a really great actress like . . ." I stopped, because no really great actress popped into my mind, but Rakosi exclaimed:

"*Eva Le Gallienne!* I can see her now, changing subtly yet unmistakably from Nina to Duchess—a moody diva furtively in love one moment; a doubting, avenging noblewoman the next. Simply terrific for Eva, of course!"

"Of course," I said. Rakosi was pleased that he let us in on what under different circumstances he would have regarded as a trade secret.

"I just had a cable from David Belasco, inquiring if I had something for Eva. This is what I call timing, boys! The right vehicle at the right time for the right star! Go on, boys. What next?"

I hadn't the faintest idea who Eva Le Gallienne was, but Rakosi's totally unexpected enthusiasm gave me wings. I had the first act sketched out in no time but managed it only by giving Eva three additional roles—those of a chambermaid; her own mother, who was a ninety-seven-year-old dipsomaniacal derelict; and an Egyptian fortuneteller whose prophecy provided the cliff-hanger for the first act curtain. Rakosi was jumping with joy.

"Terrific, boys! A truly inspired idea! A beautiful young actress like Eva suddenly turning into a ninety-seven-year-old drunken derelict. *What* a part for Le Gallienne!" He buzzed for his secretary and when she appeared he told her: "Lillian, have the boys sign contract form three-B-seven and give them four hundred pengoes. Make a note that the first act must be in not later than . . . what's today?"

"April 28, Dr. Rakosi," she said.

"Not later than September 1. That will give you plenty of time, boys, although I realize you have a difficult job with those double and quintuple parts."

"Of course," I said.

"Incidentally," Rakosi said, "what's the title of the play?"

I shot back without a moment's hesitation: *"Double or Nothing."*

"Terrific," Rakosi said, "I can see it now on the marquee, 'David Belasco Presents Eva Le Gallienne in *Double or Nothing,* a New Comedy Adapted by Ernest Hemingway.' " He said it all in a single breath, then made a sweeping move with his right arm like Lord Cardigan ordering his Light Brigade to charge: "To the barricades, boys!"

We had the first act in on time and then drew a curtain on *Double or Nothing.* Zoltan was sent by his paper to cover the Gran Chaco war in the "green hell of Bolivia," as he called the place in his dispatches. I became interested in the prosperous owner of a millinery shop on Vaci Street and had no worries for the time being about where my next meal would come from or how to assure a roof over my head.

Then came the snows and the excitement of the season in Budapest. The play stayed forgotten until one rainy afternoon in the Café New York. I was staring into a glass of black coffee hoping for someone to buy me a blue plate of cold cuts. When I looked up I found Zoltan sitting at my table. I was glad to see him because this was only the third of the month, but he was quick to disillusion me. He had blown his entire salary on Magda Kardos, the ingénue at the Chamber Theatre, and was even flatter than I was, if that were possible.

"God," he suddenly said. "Why didn't I think of it before?"

"Think of what?" I inquired.

"How long does it take you to write a second act?" he asked.

"Now look, Zoltan," I began, but he broke into my sentence: "You like to eat, don't you?"

"Of course," I said.

"You have to pay the rent, don't you?"

"Oh, yes," I said.

"Then what are you waiting for? Write the second act and all our problems are solved!"

We asked the waiter for ink, pen and paper, then called Lillian at the Rakosi office to refresh our memories. We couldn't remember at what point we had left our three characters in search of a play, or even their names. I somehow thought the soprano was called Pia, but Zoltan insisted her name was Monique. I was pleasantly surprised when Lillian told us that the soprano was called Nina because I sort of liked the name, but when she said that the duchess was Appollonia, Zoltan blew his top. "How could you think of such a corny name?" he fumed. "It sounds like one of those bottled laxatives."

"Well, what would you call her?" I said, a little piqued.

"I don't know," he said, "something sophisticated but dignified, like . . . I don't know, anything except Anasthasia."

"Appollonia," I corrected him.

"Say," he lit up, "that's not bad at all. Let's call her Appollonia."

"But . . ."

"Don't argue with me. Go to work."

We had the second act down on paper by five o'clock next morning, then went to a Turkish bath to freshen up and while away the time until we could go to Rakosi to bring about a radical improvement in our financial situation.

At ten o'clock he was reading the script.

"What do you mean, hunting lodge?" he suddenly said. "How does this hunting lodge get into the play? You told me this was a one-set production."

"Of course it is," I said quickly. "This second act is really a dream sequence. The Duke dreams he is at his hunting lodge, although he is really at . . well, exactly where he was in the first act."

Rakosi was stubborn about it. "But it says hunting lodge here! You can't make the audience dream along with him!"

"That's really very easy to fix," Zoltan broke in soothingly. "This is devised as a wonderful trick sequence. We take the chandeliers off the walls and put the stuffed heads of a couple of Bengal tigers and some gun racks in their places to create exactly the illusion we want."

"You may be right," Rakosi hesitated. "But how are you going to show that this is really a dream sequence?"

Zoltan was stumped for a moment. But he said triumphantly, "By shutting the eyes of the tigers on the wall."

I almost passed out, but Rakosi was enthusiastic.

"Say," he exclaimed, pounding Zoltan on the back, "that's cute! To tell the truth, boys, you needed a gimmick like that. I did feel the script was a bit weak gimmickwise. Incidentally," he asked, "what's the title of the play?"

Dammit, I thought, I forgot to ask Lillian. So I just said, *"The Duchess Steps Out."*

"Say," Rakosi enthused, "that's cute. How do you boys think of these titles? Of course, if Belasco wants to make it over into a melodrama, he can call it *The Duke Steps In.* Go to work, boys! I'll need the third act by September 1."

We received the second advance of 300 pengoes and then the final payment of another 300 pengoes during another acute financial crisis, which we resolved by delivering the third act way ahead of time. In the completed play, Eva Le Gallienne was called upon to play two additional parts—that of her own eleven-year-old daughter, of whose paternity she was suspecting the Duke, and that of a masseuse. But in the end we had to cut the masseuse because we couldn't figure out how Miss Le Gallienne could give herself a massage gimmickwise.

Rakosi was quite pleased even though Belasco had told him in the meantime that Eva did not think she was up to playing all those parts, including an eleven-year-old girl and, anyway, she was scheduled to go into something called *John Gabriel Borkman* by a Norwegian whose name I think was Ibsen.

The play's the thing, of course, but this particular play of ours was now a thing of the past. Rakosi never deemed it necessary to advise us of the subsequent fate of our brainchild, on the sound principle that he did not want us to get any silly ideas about becoming great playwrights.

I heard nothing of the *Green Devil*, as our play came to be titled eventually, not for some thirty years—until one night when I was watching the "Late, Late Show" on TV in New York.

Although the movie was called *Nothing for Something*, and the screen credits kept mum about Zoltan and me, I had no doubt that it was based on our play, for it followed our story line exactly, except for a single change.

Hollywood had made the star play *fifteen* different parts, gimmickwise, including one of the sleeping tiger heads on the wall.

The Eulogy

IT WAS ONLY MONDAY MORNING, BUT THE WEEK STARTED off well for Sandor Kovacs. He was awakened by a phone call from Aladar Fothy, general manager of the National Theatre, who told him that Bela Halmi had been stricken during the night and was not expected to live.

Halmi, of course, was the National's first leading man. He was a towering dramatic star, whose *Othello* of the previous season had been hailed even by Emil Jaros, Budapest's most dyspeptic drama critic, as a "historic event in the theatre, conjuring up the memory of Edmund Kean."

Kovacs, too, was a gifted and versatile actor. He had his own hits and fans, but he had the misfortune to work in the shadow of his incomparable colleague. He was referred to as Hungary's *second* greatest actor, as in Jaros' review of *Richard III,* when the stern critic wrote:

"In the title role, immortalized by Halmi's bravura performance of a couple of years ago, Sandor Kovacs came through with his usual vibrant competence, and no wonder, for he is one of our better Shakespearean actors—second maybe only to Bela Halmi himself."

Sandor Kovacs did not dislike Bela Halmi. He hated him. Hated, that is, in a purely professional sense, for he had little personal feeling for Halmi. There was no rapport between the two great stars of the National. Halmi was a lonely and morose man whose effervescence on the stage did not extend to his private personality. Lacking in charity and compassion, he was cool, curt and aloof in his pre-eminence.

Only an hour later, the phone rang again. It was Fothy calling with tears in his voice. "Oh, Sandor," he said. "I hesitate to upset you without warning because I know how fond you *were* of him—but our great Bela is no more."

Kovacs responded to the tragic news with protracted silence, letting the melodramatic silence carry its own eloquent message. During this mournful quiet he was raking up in his mind a few classic quotations from his repertory to fit the occasion. He found them in Shakespeare, of course.

"O," he began with *King John*, "amiable lovely death," but cut himself short for fear that Fothy might misconstrue the words. He switched quickly to *Richard II*.

"For God's sake," he recited with appropriate pathos, "let us sit upon the ground, and tell sad stories of the death of kings."

"So aptly put, my dear friend," Fothy said. "We have suffered an irreparable loss."

Kovacs was not so sure, but he said: "Irreparable, indeed."

He even sounded sincere and convincing, for after all, now he *was* Hungary's greatest actor at last.

"Sandor," Fothy said. "I know how filled with grief you must be. Yet you are Bela's artistic heir and so we feel that you should deliver the eulogy at our poor friend's grave. I have just discussed it with His Excellency, the Minister of

Education and Arts, and he agreed with me wholeheartedly. His Excellency will say a few words during the lying-in-state in the National's lobby, and so will I. But we expect you, my dear Sandor, to deliver the eulogy in the cemetery."

Sandor shot back in his best Hamletian tone:

"Oh, no! A thousand times no! I could not! I would be incapable of summoning the strength for so cruel an ordeal! The best flowers of mine could cast no fragrance on Bela's grave."

The phone went silent again, but only for a moment, then Kovacs said in a hushed voice, "And yet! He was my idol! When will the funeral be?"

"It is scheduled for Thursday afternoon—and thank you, dear friend. I'll let His Excellency know right away that you have consented."

Kovacs replaced the receiver and called to his wife in her bedroom. "Hilda," he said. "Halmi died. Fothy has just called; he literally begged me to deliver the eulogy."

"I'm sure you'll be great in it," she said, getting up to join her husband and kiss him on the cheek.

Then they had breakfast.

Sandor and Hilda Kovacs were the Alfred Lunt and Lynn Fontanne of Hungary, although Kovacs preferred the way Jaros once put it. On a visit to the United States during which he had seen the Lunts in *The Guardsman*, the critic described them as the "Sandor and Hilda Kovacs of America."

Hilda was a beautiful woman and a great actress in her own right. Her talent was intuitive yet overwhelming, no matter what she played. She was older than Sandor and had married him when both were at Kolozsvar in a provincial house of good repute, she already an accomplished star, he a promising young actor.

A lovely and regal actress born to play the brooding women of O'Neill, she was the perfect wife for Sandor. In his glorious masculine beauty, with his perfectly modulated, organlike voice, and his irresistible sex appeal, Kovacs was a pampered star, rampant with the usual jealousies and petulances of his kind. Unlike his wife, who was a clever woman, he was not overly quick-witted but he shrewdly concealed any want of intellect by talking elaborately with lines borrowed from his roles. He invariably managed to find a pertinent quotation for anything that popped up even in the most mundane conversation.

Hilda recognized her husband's deficiencies and catered to his vanity. She loved him with all her heart. She tactfully receded into the background and let Sandor hog the limelight.

Kovacs was one of Budapest's foremost celebrities, for the city was inordinately fond of its theatre and doted on its stars. Though it had only one-sixth of New York's population, it had as many theatres. The houses played S.R.O. almost every night, for Budapesters sought to prolong the make-believe of their days with the nocturnal fancy of the stage. They fawned upon the actors, pampered them and followed their private lives with gluttonous curiosity, copying their styles, their affectations, idiosyncrasies and manners of speech.

When once after a bibulous night, Pal Komor of the Comedy Theatre appeared in public with a black shoe on one foot and a brown shoe on the other, the young blades of Budapest promptly imitated him. They blossomed out wearing this quaint combination until Komor himself, utterly disgusted with the fad he had inadvertently created, issued a statement that it was but the product of a hangover and pleaded with his fans to return at once to the traditional style of matched footwear.

The theatre had still another important role. It supplied lovers for blasé society ladies, mistresses for men of the aristocracy and plutocracy, and paramours for the indigent but virile members of the seven arts and the fourth estate. It was perfectly institutionalized. Triangles and illicit affairs were regarded with greater respect than perfect marriages. The time that a lovely young ingénue of the Renaissance Theatre broke with her Baron, it was the Baroness herself who persuaded the girl to reconsider her decision. The Baroness was vitally interested in the maintenance of the status quo because the ingénue was leaving the Baron for the male lead of the Magyar Theatre, who happened to be the lover of the Baroness.

During a major cabinet crisis it became known that the president of the Hungarian Discount Bank had ended his liaison with the prima donna of the Royal Theatre, an enchanting singer named Hanna Haraszty. The romantic rift received bigger play in the newspapers than the political emergency.

Although he was a strange and distant Olympian figure who had produced no gossip and started no fads, Halmi had been universally admired. Now the city, informed of the sad news by extras of the afternoon papers, was shocked by his sudden death. It went into mourning with its customary zest and vim, for the death of a celebrity was always a big event in Budapest, an opportunity for splendid celebrations.

The afternoon papers had the story all over the front pages and carried long, laudatory articles about the late star. The morning papers were a bit more subdued, probably because they resented the fact that Halmi had been so inconsiderate as to die for the evening papers. But the drama page of the *Naplo,* for which Jaros wrote his penetrating reviews, appeared with a black border.

Huge black banners also were displayed on public buildings. Bela's photographs, framed in black crepe, were in all shop windows. At exactly 4 p.m., Vilmos Tarjan, manager of the Café New York, appeared on the balcony of his establishment to ask his guests to stand in silence for a minute, then order only *fekete*—the fragrant black coffee of the house—for the rest of the day.

Into this flamboyant mourning there burst further electrifying news. *Az Est,* a big afternoon paper famed for its scoops, was the first to announce it under a banner headline:

"SANDOR KOVACS AGREES TO DELIVER HALMI'S EULOGY".

It was an event of the first magnitude, one that filled Budapest's myriad theatre-lovers with great expectations, as if they were looking forward to the première of a new play by Molnar. Soon it seemed that the role Sandor Kovacs was to play at the funeral was overshadowing even Halmi's. The funeral promised to be a great artistic event.

People tiptoed as they went past the house on the ground floor of which he and Hilda had their apartment. "Shush," the passers-by said. "Be quiet!" they admonished one another. "Sandor Kovacs is working on his funeral oration."

Small bands of starry-eyed young men and women assembled under the window behind which Kovacs, visible as he paced up and down in his purple brocade dressing gown like a handsome young cardinal, dictated the eulogy to his secretary. Then came the special-events van of Radio Budapest to record a dramatic passage from the speech for the popular nightly program called *Reviews and Previews.*

The police had to be called to handle the crowd when Sandor began rehearsing the eulogy with Tamas Huvosi, senior director of the National. It was entirely Shakespeare, yet it sounded all Kovacs. His young admirers were rewarded for their vigil when fragments of the speech floated onto the street through a window that Sandor, always considerate of his fans, had left half open.

During those solemn days, Kovacs left the house only once, to motor to the Music Building on Petofi Square, where he recorded the whole eulogy for the Phoenix label.

There was a mammoth press conference the day before the funeral. Kovacs handled himself superbly, even when Zoltan Baroti from *Az Est* posed an unduly blunt question.

"Now that Bela Halmi is dead," he asked, "do you expect to get all his parts?"

A clouded expression darkened Sandor's face.

" 'Twere to consider too curiously," he answered from *Hamlet*, "to consider so. We know what we are, but we know not what we may be.' "

At last, the day of the funeral was upon Sandor Kovacs and he prepared for it with the help of his regular dresser and an extra make-up man. The cemetery was "sold out" to the last inch of standing room. Loudspeakers had been installed to carry Sandor's voice to the farthest corners.

The choir of the Municipal Theatre sang the appropriate Psalms. The Budapest Philharmonic played a few bars from the Gregorian Requiem. It was Sandor's cue. He turned to Hilda.

"How do I look?" he asked under his breath.

"Absolutely grand, sweetheart," she whispered back.

"Wish me luck." She pressed his right hand.

Kovacs mounted the pulpit and stood there, like a young Elizabethan peer—high over the open grave, the living symbol of the hoary theatrical tradition that, no matter what, the show must go on. He never looked better in his life, not even in that memorable *Richard III* after which Jaros wrote that Kovacs had finally persuaded him he was a truly gifted actor—"second maybe only to Bela Halmi. . . ."

Kovacs now recalled that review and the pain it had caused him. He looked down at the grave above which Halmi's heavy bronze casket was suspended between heaven and earth, awaiting the last savage act of interment, as if to say: "Well, Bela, here we are at last; you down there, I up here, and there is nothing either of us can do about it."

It was late in the afternoon. The huge burial place was illuminated by the golden-reddish rays of the setting sun, the soft theatrical effect of which not even Matyas Solmai, the celebrated lighting director of the National, could have improved. Suddenly, like the abrupt stab of a dagger coming from behind a heavy silken cape, Sandor's familiar voice could be heard from the loudspeakers.

"Most potent, grave and reverend seignors," he began with *King Lear*, "my very noble and approv'd good masters." He switched smoothly to *Othello*, "Rude am I in my speech, and little blessed with the soft phrase of peace," switching again, as he raised his voice, to the famous line from *Julius Caesar*, slightly edited to fit the occasion:

"I come to praise Bela Halmi, not to bury him!"

"Hear, hear," mumbled His Excellency, the Minister of Education and Arts.

"Like as waves make towards the pebbled shore," Sandor continued, "so do our minutes hasten to their end." He raised his voice again, now in a melancholy cry:

"Upon such sacrifice, o my friends . . . upon such sacrifice, the gods themselves throw incense."

He kept going, wading through *Macbeth* and *Coriolanus* and *Hamlet*, now thundering with the rage of *Richard III*, then gently intoning from *Romeo and Juliet*, "Ah, dear friends, his greatness makes this vault a feasting presence full of light."

He was coming to the end of his allotted thirty minutes and was back with *King Lear*. "Vex not his ghost," he warned, first roaring then abruptly shushing his voice to a whisper. "O! let him pass! He hates him that would upon the rack of this tough world stretch him out longer."

He surveyed the breathless crowd in which men stood enthralled and women fainted soundlessly. He paused with all the drama at his command to end with words lifted from *Henry VIII* and *Hamlet*:

"I have touched the highest point of all his greatness, and from that full meridian of my beloved friend's glory, he now hastens to his setting. Good night, sweet prince! A long farewell to all your greatness!" And then, with a final recourse to *Othello*, "And, O you mortal engines," he whispered his melodramatic punch line, "whose rude throats the immortal Jove's dread clamours counterfeit . . . Fare well!"

As if speaking the lines with him, Aladar Fothy's parched lips also moved. He, too, was reciting a passage from *Othello:* "O! beware my lord of jealousy, the green-eyed monster which doth mock the meat it feeds on."

But nobody, not even the Minister of Education and Arts, who sat next to him, could hear Fothy's words—and now it was all over. Sandor Kovacs stood in the pulpit, his head bowed, his body crumbled from the exhaustion of his magnificent effort, tears streaming from his eyes. Now nobody could doubt it any longer—*he* was Hungary's greatest actor.

Then something eerie and strange happened. It began spontaneously and quietly, only here and there, then it welled up like a mighty clamor. The audience between the graves and the tombstones and mausoleums was clapping hands, stamping feet and shouting over the din of the deafening applause: "Bravo! Bravo! Encore! Bravo!"

Poor Bela Halmi slipped into his cold grave as this roar of applause resounded, the forgotten man of this unprecedented event in the theatrical history of Hungary.

Sandor Kovacs sat silently at Hilda's side in the big black limousine that drove them home from his triumph in the cemetery. He appeared to be deep in thought and Hilda did not want to disturb him, not even with her praise. Then abruptly Sandor came to life. He turned to his wife and asked her:

"Tell me, Hilda, do you think I could go on the road with this eulogy?"

The Prince and the Ballerina

AS A YOUNG REPORTER I WORKED FOR A MAN WHOM I SHALL call Arpad Vas who owned and edited a weekly morning newspaper that more or less monopolized the field, since no other paper in Budapest was published the same day. Vas specialized in what he called intimate scoops, culling them from suppressed police blotters, digging them up in the darkest recesses of the city's vivacious café society or making them up. He preferred intimate scoops of the third category for three reasons. "You see," he once told me, "when you print a good story that you make up yourself you are sure you have a good story to begin with. Later it is denied and you have the story a second time. And, thirdly, it is exclusive."

Once, when he was really hard up for an intimate scoop, he hired a starving young actor to attempt to seduce his, Vas's, wife. Then he hired another starving young actor to beat up the would-be seducer in the Café New York at 9:00 p.m., when the place was crowded, insisting that he had first mort-

58

gage on Mrs. Vas's affections. It made a hell of a good story for page one and then it made a second story when Mrs. Vas eloped one day with one of the actors for real. And it was exclusive, too.

I was only a cub reporter, to be sure, handling mostly bizarre stories like the suicide attempted by a celebrated gambler over a chorus girl named Mitzi Horvath. He didn't really want to kill himself; he merely wanted to impress Mitzi. Otherwise he would have used a more lethal weapon than the four loaded dice he swallowed. The story became big when the gambler died unexpectedly and the autopsy revealed that the dice he swallowed had been dipped into hydrocyanic acid. The case was never solved.

I was only a cub, as I said before, and I was somewhat surprised, therefore, when Vas called me into his office and told me: "Listen, son, I have the makings of an intimate scoop here but it needs a little leg work. I was tipped off that someone is shopping around town for a mistress for young Prince Esterhazy. He's about to come of age and has to be brought up to date on the birds and the bees. Go get me that story and I'll give you a nice bonus."

I took the bull by the horns and went straight to the forbidding Esterhazy palace on a sleepy, cobblestoned old street in Buda. I was received by the young Prince's secretary, a courteous priest, and I confronted him with the question point-blank: "This is my biggest assignment to date, Father," I told him, "and I'd really appreciate it if you'd give me some help. Is it true that someone is shopping for a mistress for His Grace and, if yes, who is doing the shopping, where is the shopping being done and why?"

The secretary flashed his friendliest smile, then said with exquisite courtesy: "Please wait a moment." He rang a bell and told the husky young footman who answered it: "Janos, please throw this gentleman out."

The order was carried out so promptly and vigorously that I needed three stitches in my face, on which I landed. This was nothing unusual. I needed seven stitches after I went to ask Albert Brill whether it was true that he had embezzled 400,000 pengoes from the bank of which he was president.

Never discouraged by initial difficulties, I went after the story from another angle and soon had my first lead. I got it from the young footman who had thrown me out. I accosted him on his day off and gave him twenty pengoes under the table at Imre's beer joint.

"Try the opera," he said.

"What opera," I asked, not being a musicophile.

"You know," he said, "the big one on Andrassy Avenue."

This was, then, in the grand tradition of Hungarian aristocracy—shopping for a mistress at the Royal Hungarian Opera House. Its very romance warmed my heart, for in Hungary even clandestine Communists had a soft spot for the country's titled nobility.

The nobility was a spectacularly feudal society with both feet firmly planted in the past, paying no attention to the forward march of democracy, much less social democracy. Hungary no longer had a king—its chief of state was an admiral named Horthy who had the title of *kormanyzo,* or Regent—but the old court remained almost intact.

The aristocracy consisted of the landed gentry occupying the lowest rung of the ladder, the barons, the counts, the princes, and a few royal dukes thrown in for good measure in that order. They lived in a sort of fairyland like King Arthur's court as Mark Twain saw it—in their elegant town houses, on their huge country estates, in their summer homes on Lake Balaton, spending their winters either at Davos and St. Moritz or in their villas on the Riviera. They were tailored by Savile Row, but on festive occasions they appeared in the elaborate costumes of their ancestors, trimmed with priceless furs. They had their limousines and swank sports cars but they preferred to be drawn by horses, in gigs or tallyhos or six-in-hand landaus with coachmen and footmen up in front.

They were surrounded by their own courts and small armies of servants, including butlers, valets, footmen, chefs, scullery maids, upstairs maids, laundresses, coachmen, grooms, tutors and, especially, governesses. The latter, imported mostly from a city called Graz in Austria, usually were pretty young ladies who served several purposes. They took excellent care of the smaller children, introduced the bigger boys to the facts of life, and slept with the lords of the manors in certain emergencies, such as times when no other companionship was immediately available and her ladyship was not in residence.

It would have been very simple for the mighty Esterhazys to convey the facts of life to the young Prince at home because he, too, had his quota of governesses from Graz and they had the reputation of being the most charming and the prettiest in Buda. But the Esterhazys were Hungary's premier nobles, who stuck most conservatively to the customs of the past. Under their own house rules, a hereditary prince was to remain a virgin until his twenty-first birthday, when he was given all sorts of expensive gifts, including a mistress.

The young lady was chosen with extraordinary care, was then endowed with a monthly apanage, put up in a lovely apartment of her own, and kept under surveillance by spies planted in the establishment in the guise of chambermaids. Such liaisons often endured; there was one Esterhazy in the nineteenth century who divorced five wives but remained true to his first mistress to the end of his life.

The Prince was an exceptionally handsome and pleasant young man. He was lean, tall and nobly limbed, a thoroughbred prince in every respect. He had blond hair, powder-blue eyes and a peachy complexion, yet he didn't look effeminate because his serene face, with its finely carved nose, ample lips and well-rounded, firm jaw gave him a distinctly masculine appearance. He was also reputed to be far different from the jejune young men of his caste—most of them brainless fops. He had just been graduated with honors from a famous German agricultural academy where he studied for his major mission in life, the administration of his two million acres.

The Esterhazys were once world-famous as music lovers and Hungary's foremost patrons of that art. In the eighteenth century, the great Austrian composer Franz Joseph Haydn served for twenty-nine years as their musical director, and Franz Liszt also benefited from their lavish munificence. This devotion to music apparently moved the family even in the selection of mistresses. They were often pretty, young sopranos at the threshold of their career, sometimes a harpist or zitherist, but ballerinas were invariably chosen to start things off.

Knowing the tradition of the house, I realized at once that Janos the footman had put me on the right track when he steered me to the Opera. Discreet inquiries accompanied by the customary bribes rewarded me with the very information I was seeking. A few days before, I was told, a delegation of high-ranking Esterhazy retainers had called on Geza Barany, the director-general of the Opera House. The spokesman confided to Director Barany that they were looking for an accomplished member of the Corps de Ballet—not a *première danseuse* by any means but a simple little ballet girl whose accomplishments had to include youth, beauty and a pleasing disposition. She had to be a tall, slender blonde with blue eyes and a creamy skin (presumably to complement the downy complexion of the Prince).

This was an historic event, one that occurred only once in many years, whenever a princely heir of the House of Esterhazy came of age. The last time such a delegation had been at the Opera on a similar errand had been forty-five years earlier, when a ballerina had to be chosen for the Prince's father. The second or third sons of the house had no hereditary right to ballerinas and had to be satisfied with young ladies from the music halls.

The presence of the committee set the Corps de Ballet on fire. When the specifications became known inside the house, all the girls blossomed out as ash-blondes overnight. They also treated their lovely skins with all sorts of potions and lotions to make them look creamy.

But they could not fool Director Barany. He knew that there was only a single ash-blonde, blue-eyed girl in the whole Corps de Ballet who also happened to be tall, slender and have a creamy complexion and a pleasant disposition—in short, the ideal Cinderella for this Prince Charming.

She was Melinda Vago, the nineteen-year-old daughter of the Chief Doorman of the Opera House. Melinda was a well-known young beauty of Budapest, and not only on her own merits. She was even better known as Uncle Vago's pretty little daughter. Her father happened to be one of the city's authentic landmarks.

Uncle Vago was a huge, broad-shouldered, formidable man who looked like a forbidding character out of an opera by Richard Wagner. His appearance was made even more menacing by an enormous beard that covered his face and flowed slowly down to his impressive chest. He was on display every night on the steps of the main entrance of the Opera House on Andrassy Avenue, the floodlights of the house illuminating his striking figure as he stood erect like a giant *tannen* tree, holding his big oaken staff away from him in a majestic gesture—looking straight ahead as the opera-goers swarmed past him.

His Melinda was discreetly viewed by members of the delegation and they voted her in unanimously. Now all that was left to be done was to discuss the matter with Uncle Vago, since a dutiful young daughter like Melinda had no choice of her own in these matters.

Uncle Vago was summoned into Director Barany's office and the proposition was presented to him with all its attractive trimmings. What followed resembled a scene from *Samson et Delilah,* where the eyeless giant of Gaza shakes the pillars and brings down the palace. Uncle Vago drew himself up to his entire enormous height and told the assembled gentlemen to go and get themselves another ballerina because his Melinda was not available for such sordid purposes. Only he said it more forcefully.

That seemed to end the search because the delegation, thus touched by this mighty gale of paternal indignation, fled from the premises, realizing at last that the times had changed and ballerinas were no longer to be had in the open market.

I had my story straight and my efforts blossomed out as an intimate scoop the next morning in Arpad Vas's paper. Apparently it wrote finis to the whole affair because I heard nothing more and could not even get enough data for a follow-up. Nothing happened with the Prince for another year, except that he came of age and, upon his father's death during that year, became the head of the house.

Then he suddenly supplied an intimate item that made the front pages of every newspaper in Budapest and so, unhappily, was no scoop for us. It came to my desk in the form of a release penned by Father Gyenes that read: "The Princess Esterhazy de Kismarton is pleased to announce the engagement of her son to Miss Melinda Vago, only daughter of Mr. Jozsef Vago."

The announcement shook the earth under me because Arpad Vas led a one-man stampede to my desk, shaking a fist at me and yelling: "You idiot, you wretched fool! How could you have missed this intimate scoop?"

I was flabbergasted, then went out on my own to discover

how I could have missed it, indeed. My chagrin became even greater when I discovered that in a very real sense I was the unknowing matchmaker behind the engagement. What had happened was this:

When my story about that crisis in Director Barany's office in the Opera House appeared in the paper, the young Prince happened to read it, although frantic efforts were made at the Palais Esterhazy to conceal the "scandal" from him. Far from being annoyed or embarrassed, he was amused and, indeed, intrigued.

He himself called Barany to inquire when Melinda would next appear on the stage and when he was told that it would be in the next performance of Gautier's *Giselle* on Tuesday, he instructed Father Gyenes to buy for him loge number 1, the closest to the stage. He appeared more or less incognito, never took his opera glasses off Melinda, and liked what he saw enormously. The next morning, he penned a little note to Melinda, congratulating her on her performance and apologizing for the embarrassment he had unwittingly caused.

Melinda responded in a gracious letter and soon she was meeting the Prince *a deux* at a little *confiserie* in Buda, not far from the Palais Esterhazy, where they indulged themselves with *café melange* and cream puffs. It may sound somewhat corny, but what can you do? These young people fell in love to the point that they could no longer live apart. The Prince took his plight to his mother, the Dowager Princess, and told her he would never marry in his life unless he were allowed to take Melinda as his bride. The Dowager gave her consent immediately because, you see, she, too, had been a ballerina before she married the Prince's father.

I
Love You
in Greek

HAVE YOU EVER BEEN IN LOVE WITH A HUNGARIAN CHORUS girl named Ancy who was fond of *Coulibiac de saumon á l'Escoffier* with hot Sauce Bercy, a dazzling thirty-dollar dish —the Coulibiac, I mean—which could be purchased only at Gundel's, the best restaurant in Budapest?

You have?

Then you will readily understand why I had to leave town overnight and go all the way to Berlin, telling Ancy in a tearful farewell note that I simply adored her but couldn't afford to share her with Monsieur Escoffier.

In Berlin I met girls who liked sauerbraten and Königsberger klops, but unfortunately I couldn't afford them either. I was looking for a girl who was either on a diet or who would love me for myself.

I tried to make a living by writing lyric poetry in Hungarian and was baffled when I couldn't sell my poems in Germany. Where I hoped to gain fame I found only famine.

Finally came what I feared was the collapse of my hungry dawns in Berlin. I was returning home at what I called my witching hour, because my rent was four or five months in arrears and the old witch in whose flat I lived would get tired, around 3 a.m., of sitting up for me. When she had gone to bed at last I could sneak into the apartment. I had to be out again by not later than seven, but even a few hours of sleep in my own bed was better than spending the night in a railroad station waiting room.

Now it was three, but when I tiptoed into the apartment in my stocking feet, feeding a bone to the dog, I found that my precautions were wasted. The apartment was all lit up. A couple of feminine voices could be heard in the parlor. Then my landlady—wide awake—burst into the corridor, catching me *in flagrante*.

"I'm so sorry, Frau Stuckenschmidt," I mumbled, "but I can assure you that by next Monday . . ."

She didn't seem to hear me as she said:

"Oh, there you are, dear boy, how nice to see you? And so chipper at this early hour. Where have you been? We've been waiting for you simply for hours. Come in, dear boy, and join in the fun!"

I was dumfounded. She hadn't spoken to me so kindly since the day I took her wretched back room and gave her two months' rent in advance. It was obvious that what made her drip with the milk of human kindness didn't come from a cow. It came from a distillery. She was positively plastered.

"Ancy!"

The horrible thought abruptly flashed through my mind! That other voice in the parlor! It sounded like Ancy's voice. She must be here! Nobody else in the whole wide world could make my landlady so blissful and drunk at half past three in the morning!

I staggered into the living room and there she was, with

glass in hand, in all her splendor. She greeted me with a moving toast:

"Hi, bum!"

Yes, it was good old Ancy. She had come to Berlin, allegedly after me, but really in search of greener pastures. She
had arrived on the 7:00 train at the Anhalter Station and had
come straight to my abode, the only terra firma she knew of
in the strange city.

She had a mystic knack of making people like her and
bend to her whims. As if mesmerized by her *savoir vivre,* they
went along with her on the craziest tangents, out on the most
precarious limbs. She had taken my landlady by storm, then
settled down with her to the night's long vigil over ample re-
freshments. She gave old Stuckenschmidt the best time of her
life—by some strange osmosis, because my landlady spoke
only German and Ancy could speak nothing but Hungarian.

Ancy had an amazing vocabulary entirely her own, re-
splendent with one-syllable, four-letter words like: mink and
jew'l and crap—and also the less socially acceptable kind,
which she bandied about with such impish innocence that
everything she said sounded very nice, indeed. She was a virtuoso of her special lingo. It was—after her pretty face, excellent figure and considerable erudition in bed—her greatest
asset.

In Hungary no man could resist her vernacular, but this
being Germany, where an entirely different tongue was spoken,
I feared Ancy might have to fall back on her face or figure,
or, indeed, on her erudition in bed.

But apparently language was no barrier to this girl! She
talked an unending stream to my landlady, who actually
laughed at the right places although she could not have understood any of Ancy's off-color lines.

Well, we lived happily ever after—while Ancy's money
lasted, that is—and then a few days more from the proceeds

of the return part of her two-way ticket, which we cashed in at a travel bureau. But when we had to fall back on my resources and Ancy realized there was no future in lyric poetry, she checked out to start in earnest her search for those greener pastures.

I used to see her once in a while in the Café Hessler, a cosmopolitan hangout of show folk, writers, painters and rich stage-door Johnnies. She could be seen cuddled up to the latter, talking to them in Hungarian all the time and making them eat out of her hand although it was obvious they couldn't understand a word she said—just the physical Esperanto she exuded.

She stubbornly refused to learn German and maybe it was just as well, because she got along formidably with her effusive Hungarian gibberish. It even lent her an Oriental charm of linguistic mystery. She must have been doing all right, insofar as I could judge from a growing accumulation of mink, jew'ls and other such accessories that adorned her lithe body.

Suddenly she vanished without a trace.

I had heard nothing from her for almost a year when one disenchanted morning I found in my mail, along with a couple of rejection slips, a gold and blue embossed invitation. His Excellency the Ambassador of Greece requested the pleasure of my company for tea on the afternoon of May the Fifteenth.

Written in her childish scrawl at the bottom of the card was a message from Ancy: "Lissen, you bum, I'd be glad to feedya provided you gotta tie."

I reported at the service entrance at the appointed hour, convinced that Ancy must be one of the upstairs maids at the Embassy and that the embossed invitation was a practical joke. But the staid butler who opened the back door told me: "Mademoiselle and His Excellency are expecting you, sir, at the Residence."

It was Ancy in the flesh who stood at the top of a huge

staircase in an ornate big hall. She was dressed in a *soigné* cocktail dress from Helene's. Her auburn hair was coiffed by Albert of the Eden. She had a Cartier assortment on her fingers, her wrist and around her satin neck. She was the picture of pulchritude and prosperity.

But it was the old Ancy who yelled down to me: "Hiya, bum! So whattya say?"

I said nothing because I was speechless. When I recovered I meekly asked: "What's this, a hoax or something?"

"Shuddup," said she. "I'm having a little *geshpoosie* with His Schnookie-Pootzie the Ambassador and I thought you might wanna see the setup."

At that historic moment, Schnookie-Pootzie himself appeared at the top of the stairs. He was a tall debonair man in his late fifties, with slickly groomed black hair graying at the temples and a ruddy complexion. He had an austere yet kindly look behind a pair of horn-rimmed glasses. He was all dressed up for the occasion in Savile Row black jacket and the regulation striped pants.

Ancy bussed him condescendingly—to which he responded with the sheepish gratitude of a lapdog being patted on the head—then she introduced him to me:

"This is the bum, Schnookie, I told you I used to starve with in Budapest."

She said it in Hungarian and from the vague smile on His Excellency's face I could see at once that he didn't understand a single syllable. He came down the stairs, shook my hand, said in impeccable diplomatic French: "I am so pleased to meet you at last. Mademoiselle told me so much about you."

I must have looked at him like a rube because he added quickly: "Oh, it does not really matter that I do not speak Hungarian. Did not Shakespeare say: 'There's language in her eye, her cheek, her lip'?"

I thought he was a nice guy, but Ancy asked with a touch of hostility in her voice: "What'd he tellya?"

When I translated the gallant remark, she asked suspiciously: "Whattya think he meant, the bastard?"

"It was a sweet compliment, Ancy," I soothed her.

"Don't try to pull anything on me in your friggin' French, you two!" she warned, and kicked the Ambassador in his left shin. She was rewarded with a tolerant smile from His Excellency and an ethereal kiss on her beautiful forehead.

Tea was served on genuine *pâte tendre* Sèvres porcelain with the Embassy's Regency silver in the cozy Blue Room under a priceless Louis Quatorze tapestry. I was seated next to the marble torso of a nude Greek woman of antiquity.

"You know what Schnookie-Pootzie always tells me?" Ancy pointed at the torso. "He says I got tits like her."

The Ambassador was gently interested.

"What did mademoiselle say?" he asked.

"Oh," I said, gasping for words. "She just mentioned that torso here, because . . . because it reminds her of Praxiteles with the elegance of its proportions and its sensuous beauty."

"How keen!" His Excellency exclaimed. "How exquisitely keen! I didn't realize she knew so much about the ancient art of my country. I'm delighted, truly delighted! And she wasn't too far off, even in her timing. The torso is attributed to Myron, who was more or less a contemporary of Praxiteles."

Ancy sat there, slightly bewildered.

"Didya tell'im by any chance what I said about the stater?" she asked, and I said: "Yes, up to a point." She laughed uproariously.

"It kills me! He's so bashful, the old spooner! You know, he always insists we turn off the lights before we make love."

His Excellency raised an expectant eyebrow, waiting for the simultaneous interpretation. I was stumped for a moment.

"Mademoiselle quoted Lytton," I stammered desperately,

"where he says that sculptor on sculptor must have starved with the thought in the head by the hand uncarved."

A broad smile came on the Ambassador's serene face.

"Ah, yes," he replied, "a beautiful line from *Babylonia*," and he completed the stanza. He was a man of some erudition himself.

"How *magnifique!*" he said. "How perfectly *magnifique!* I must say I've adored my dear Ancy even across this confounded language barrier. But you're opening up new vistas, dear friend. New vistas."

And so it went, for the rest of the afternoon.

I was asked to stay for dinner, just *à trois*, because His Excellency could not get enough of Ancy's universal genius as she discoursed on the Treaty of Tilsit, "that milestone in diplomatic history," on Il Moretto, the sixteenth-century Italian painter of the Brescia school, on the races at Chantilly and on Schoenberg's atonal music, on the Geological Survey of the United States and on the legal validity of a gentleman's agreement.

The high point of this linguistic triangular marathon was reached when Ancy suddenly told me: "You can't stay too long, ya bum, because my Schnookie-Pootzie runs on a strict timetable. He wants me in his bed no later than ten o'clock. He needs a coupla hours to work up his passion."

I translated with perfect fluency by then: "Mademoiselle said the music of ancient Greece must have been a highly developed art, even if it was entirely monodic, because each mode was associated with a definite type of emotion according to the doctrine of ethos."

The Ambassador was nonplussed.

"How does she know these things?" he asked, and I turned to Ancy. "Say something, anything, but quick!"

"—— you," she said quietly.

"From the third book of Plato's *Republic*," I translated.

Cognac and coffee were served in His Excellency's private study, for just the two of us, because the Ambassador wanted to be alone with me. He bade me sit down on a big Chippendale sofa, seemed to hesitate as if pondering something, then turned to me.

"As our great Aeschylus said," he began, "words are the physicians of a mind diseased. Today I have heard words that have assuaged my troubled mind. Perhaps I need not tell you that I am deeply in love with our dear Ancy. Yet I had my doubts—such gnawing, harrowing doubts—because our inability to communicate in a common tongue prevented me from penetrating to her inner soul."

He stood up, took a deep breath and told me:

"I wonder if I could ask you to do me the honor of proposing to mademoiselle on my behalf?"

While until this fateful moment I had felt a little like Pygmalion, now suddenly it dawned upon me that I was closer to Dr. Frankenstein. I tried frantically to warn His Excellency with another hastily summoned quotation from his own favorite, Aeschylus:

"I'd far rather be ignorant than wise in the foreboding of evil."

But he was adamant! Ancy was summoned. She came, already undressed for action (for it was past ten o'clock) in a sexy black Venetian nightgown. When I asked her to marry His Excellency, she nearly fainted. But she recovered swiftly to ask: "Why the hell does he wanna marry me?"

The thought seemed to be bothering her, even when I said: "Because apparently he loves you dearly."

"Oh, bullfeathers," she returned with a charming smile. "Mebbe he thinks he can get me cheaper when I'm his missus. You can never tell with 'em Greeks!"

"Mademoiselle is overwhelmed and honored," I said solemnly, "and her answer, of course, is a delighted yes."

They spent their honeymoon cruising in His Excellency's yacht in the Aegean Sea and in his villa on Soriphes, one of the Cyclades. Then the Ambassador was appointed to a high post in the Foreign Ministry and they went to live in Athens. The letters Ancy wrote to me from there were exuberant. For the first time, I thought, they reflected a new trait in her—sincere gratitude.

In the meantime, I moved on to Paris and lived there under rather strained circumstances in a small hotel in the rue de Champollion on the Left Bank. I spent much of my genius on efforts to evade the concierge, much in the manner in which I used to elude Frau Stuckenschmidt.

One morning at four, as I tried to skulk unnoticed into the hotel, I found my path blocked by piles of elegant luggage that made the hall resemble the baggage room of a railroad station. Sleeping between two tall piles of chamois suitcases were three Pekingese of an eccentric variety. There was also a huge parrot in a gilded cage.

The concierge emerged from her cubby hole at my sight and said: "Madam is in the royal suite on the third floor. She instructed me to ask monsieur to call on her no matter how late."

It was Ancy, of course; a more mature, more beautiful and, somehow it seemed to me, a much wiser Ancy.

"I'm getting a divorce," she told me simply.

"I'm so sorry," I said. "What happened?"

"I really don't know," she mused. Then she told me with a new melancholy undertone in her voice: "Everything seemed to be just fine—too good to be true, in fact. He had a darling little ole mother and a spinster sister, and they took to me like ducks to water. For the first time in my darn life I felt, I don't know how—so safe, so cozy. I decided to surprise my husband on our first wedding anniversary with something he wanted so badly. I learned to speak Greek."

"Oh," I said.

The Colonel's Baby and Other Women at Work

BABY KISS WAS THE STAR PUPIL OF THE GRADUATING CLASS at the Girls' Lycée in Budapest, a finishing school named after Katicza Dobo, a popular heroine of old Hungary who once led a band of Amazons against the Turks.

Baby was even more popular than Katicza, for several reasons. First of all, Katicza has long been dead, while Baby was very much alive. And, secondly, while Katicza was in favor of resisting the enemy, Baby was all for surrendering to him.

In the immediate wake of the war, when things were hard to get, she would surrender for a cake of soap, a pair of nylon hose, or a carton of cigarettes. But it wasn't long before she was getting a mink coat or a diamond ring for exactly the same sort of surrender that used to bring her a mere Hershey bar.

Baby was barely eighteen years old and still at school when she discovered that she had a special appeal to the enemy troops. After that, she became so busy with her homework that

75

she had no more time for school. When once she stayed away from her classes because of a minor operation and her principal found out that it had been of an illicit variety, Baby was told that formal education could teach her nothing more.

She did not miss school. She had already found her true mission in life—the American Military Mission. By then she was so smart that she could tell a major's oak leaf from a colonel's eagle, a knowledge that helped her enormously to get along in the world even without a diploma from the Girls' Lycée named after Katicza Dobo.

I met Baby Kiss twice—first in her native habitat in Budapest shortly after the war, when she was at the peak of her popularity, and then, about a decade later, in the lobby of the St. Regis in New York, where she was accompanied by a nice middle-aged man under a ten-gallon hat. She seemed to be very popular with him, too. I liked her very much because she symbolized to me the epitome of one kind of Hungarian woman at her scintillating best, a delightful quality whose stirring *je ne sais quoi* did so much to make my own youth in Hungary such a felicitous experience.

To say that Baby was very beautiful is not only stating the obvious but considerably understating it. Her beauty was a mystic mixture of all sorts of esthetic qualities, some innate, some acquired. She was terrific, medium large everywhere, the kind of economy size that makes men forget their economies.

She had a few tricky features that showed off her ornaments to better advantage—seven cute little freckles, for example. They went into a merry dance whenever she wrinkled her nice little nose or twittered her nostrils, tickled by bubbles of champagne. Her skin was smooth and white like fine-grained marble, with thin, pale-amethyst veins lending it a lavender hue. She walked with a springy gait, her shapely buttocks swinging right and left in a rhythmic wig-wag the choreography of which was one of her trade secrets.

She was forever gay, just this side of being vulgar, chattering in a husky voice, laughter rolling like pearls from her lips. She oozed good cheer and held out the promise of a corking good time, a promise she kept with such ecstatic abandon that the men who became the beneficiaries of her charity were enraptured with her all over again each time she treated them to the full sweep of her generosity.

In other words, Baby was just a typical Hungarian woman.

There were hundreds of them like Baby adrift in Budapest, spreading the *joie de vivre* with a know-how so consummate and ingratiating that it made the dreary task of occupying a defeated country a delectable chore indeed.

Baby and the other girls of her sorority were not blazing a trail by any means. Although she was far too young to know it, she was merely helping history repeat itself.

After World War I, too, there was an American Military Mission briefly in Hungary to share in the occupation of the country. But after looking the country over, the Americans decided to occupy merely the Ritz Hotel. The Mission was so small, in fact, that it had to borrow someone from the British Military Mission whenever it needed a fourth for bridge. The highest-ranking Yank in town was a captain, but he was so stunningly turned out and had his high cavalry boots so brilliantly polished that the natives mistook him for a general. As a matter of fact, he looked much smarter than the Rumanian field marshal who was the dean of the occupation forces.

Firmly entrenched in the Ritz, the American captain quickly realized that—what with his limited forces and powers—he would have to be very selective in his aid to the devastated little country. So he picked a single Hungarian to rehabilitate. She was a most deserving young woman, badly in need of rehabilitation because she had never had any furs and jewels of her own, and had never been inside the Ritz until the good-hearted American captain sheltered her there.

Her name was Margit, but she changed it to Peggy to accommodate her benefactor and did everything else she could to make the captain's life in Budapest agreeable. When once a colonel from the Inspector General's office arrived in Budapest to check up on the progress of the American rehabilitation program, he was amazed at how well the captain had managed his job. He was most impressed with how well Peggy looked, how well she was fed and housed, for he didn't expect, even in his fondest dream, that a little waif like Peggy would have a sable coat and dresses from Paris so soon after the war.

Baby Kiss was far too young to remember Peggy but she did not need any historical precedents to know how to conduct herself. She was a typical woman of Budapest and operated entirely on instinct. Thus her instinct told her that an American colonel was worth five Russian generals and that the dollar was a more stable currency than the pound sterling. She got herself a job tending bar at the Park Club, where the American officers had their mess. After first testing her allure on a second lieutenant and then practicing on a couple of majors, she cuddled up to her colonel.

When the Americans first arrived in Budapest, they were reasonably certain that they alone had won the war. After a while they weren't so sure. First the Russians got into the act and then it became evident that if anybody had won the war it was Baby Kiss.

The colonel Baby hooked was no dreamboat. As a matter of fact, he was only five feet three and it took a world war as well as a special dispensation from the Pentagon to transfer him from the National Guard to the regular army. His head was far too big, his legs were far too short and he was as bald as a bowling ball. He told Baby he was from somewhere in Oklahoma and he entertained her, when they had nothing better to do, with fancy rope tricks and wild tales about the broncos, whatever they were. He was also quite open-handed and supplied Baby with everything she needed, and some things she didn't need at all, such as an original painting of the Gallic War, an ivory chess set and twenty-four volumes of the Encyclopaedia Britannica. But, then, what are you going to give a girl who has everything?

From what the colonel told her, Baby assumed that her little officer must be a big shot back in Oklahoma. He would tell her grandly about his farm and of the things he used to do in Beaver County as if he owned it, the whole county, that is. Baby wasn't too wise about those things. Her idea of Oklahoma stemmed mostly from Rodgers and Hammerstein via the USO.

Hardboiled though Baby was, she did have dreams, the gilt-edged variety. Now she visualized a huge tract of rich, rolling land in Oklahoma, with acres of corn as high as an elephant's eye, plenty of horses and cattle, a big colonial mansion with slender pillars in front and servants scurrying to and fro. She saw herself as the little woman of the big house, riding around the farm in a surrey with a fringe on top.

The little colonel put her up in style in a cozy little villa on a tree-lined, broad *allée* in Budapest from whose elegant houses the Nazis had just been evicted. He hired an upstairs maid and a cook for her and took her horseback-riding on the bridle path of the Bois early in the morning. While the colonel was busy in the office, Baby saw her dressmakers and milliners, had herself measured for shoes and fur coats, and went to the beauty parlor to have her auburn hair tinted a flaming red that went exquisitely with her smooth alabaster skin.

Baby wasn't usually grateful. She thought anyway that this was an equitable *quid pro quo*. But one night, thinking in her bed, she sat up and, without any apparent reason, kissed the colonel softly on his forehead.

"What's the matter, honey?" he asked, a little surprised because it wasn't Baby's regular habit to kiss him without any apparent reason and sometimes the reason had to be two karats or more.

"I was just thinking," she said, "how good you are to me."

"That's all right, honey," the colonel soothed her. Then he added cryptically: "You may not realize it, Baby, but you've earned every bit you got."

One day there was a sudden change. It all began when a couple of stern-faced officers flew in from Washington, had a long talk with the general behind closed doors and were closeted for hours with the colonel. After that Baby could hardly keep up with the rush of events, everything was happening so fast.

The colonel came home for lunch as usual, but he was not alone. He brought with him the chaplain of the Mission and told Baby:

"You know the padre, don't you, honey? Well, let's have a bite and then, if you're free, we can get spliced."

In no time, the colonel's Baby became the colonel's wife. That same night the colonel took off his uniform and packed it away in his footlocker, then packed everything else he had, including his collection of priceless embroideries, the 584-piece china set he had found in an abandoned castle, the Rembrandt he had salvaged from the ruins of the bombed-out Museum of Fine Arts, all the little loot he had traced down, dug up, ferreted out or just plain stole, now filling a dozen crates. Next morning the little colonel and his new missus flew out of Budapest. They spent a week in Paris, a couple of days in Washington, then non-stop to the farm in Oklahoma.

Baby was bewildered by the rush and didn't like the setup. She thought the little colonel looked funny and coarse in his new civvies, under his oversized Stetson. But her real surprise was still in store for her. It was the farm! Rodgers and Hammerstein must have been mad when they set to music all that twaddle about Oklahoma. "Oh, what a beautiful morning," my eye.

Their feudal estate, not far from Logan, was straight out of John Steinbeck. The farm was a few acres of barren land, smack in the heart of the Dust Bowl. They were greeted by a sand storm wafting in thick, dark grit that smothered everything from the crops and the pasturage to the sofa in the ramshackle wreck that was called the house.

"Is this your place, Pitzi?" she asked.

"Yeah," the little guy said. "But don't you worry, honey. We can go to Beaver on Saturdays, the county seat. It's only twenty miles away. You'll like it, Baby. Beaver is real nice." Then he changed his tone abruptly:

"But if you don't like it, honey, there's a bus out of Logan tomorrow at two o'clock in the afternoon. It'll take you down to Oklahoma City, where you can catch a plane for New York. And I won't be blaming you a bit, honey."

She sat down on the dust-covered sofa and buried her head in her hands, her whole body shaking with her wail of woe. The little guy let her cry, but after a while he went over to her, put a soft hand on her bobbing shoulder and said mildly: "You must be famished, hon. I'll whip up a coupla eggs for you. How about it, Baby?"

She got up, went to him and shouted: "Why did you marry me?"

"I had to, honey," the little guy said quietly.

"I don't understand."

"You see, hon, those characters who flew in from Washington were from JAG, the Judge Advocate General's office. They were after us."

"What do you mean *us?*"

"I was playing the black market a little, to get you all those nice things, hon, and was making a few fast bucks with scrip. Those characters had nothing on me, because I did everything in your name, honey, and they'd have had something on you only if I testified against you.

"I had to do some fast footwork. I grabbed the padre on the way home and got hitched to you, hon. We had no time to lose, don't you see?"

"No time to lose?" Baby was bitter and desperate.

"Yeah," the little guy said. "They'd have come for you in the afternoon, but I told 'em, what's the use? A husband can't be made to testify against his wife, that's what the law says. And now I was your husband, see. I had to take you off the hook, kid, or you'd be in some clink in Budapest right now instead of the Dust Bowl."

The little guy gave her money—all the cash he had left.

"I can't give you the Rembrandt, honey," he explained. "It's too hot. And what would you want with all that goddam china? Maybe you wanna go back to Budapest. I'll send you the annulment by registered mail, hon. Just let me know where you'll be."

There was a momentary silence in that dismal room. Then the little guy said: "Well, it was swell while it lasted, Baby. It's no use cryin' over spilt milk, honey, that's what I always say."

But Baby cried, for suddenly she realized that—with all her sophistication and wisdom in the ways of the world, with all her built-in instinct and her rapacious talent for the slick squeeze—she was the yokel who got caught, not the little hick from the Dust Bowl.

The bus was five hours late out of Logan and so she missed the plane in Oklahoma City. Waiting for the next one, she looked around and saw the horizon darkened by rows and rows of strange contraptions like inverted cones.

"What are those towers over there?" she asked a stranger under a ten-gallon hat who was sitting next to her and chewing gum as if his life depended on it.

"Them?" the stranger said. "Derricks. Oil wells."

"Don't tell me," she said, "that this horrible place is making oil!"

"You're damn right, ma'am," the man said, "that this is a horrible place, plain horrible, as you say. I'm from Texas myself, and where are you from, if I ain't intruding?"

"From Budapest."

"Never heard of it, ma'm, but it must be a mighty fine place if they're turning 'em out as perty as you are."

So that was how it came to pass that the colonel's Baby became president of the PTA of the James Bowie Junior High School in Fort Worth, Texas.

Just One More Bottle of Champagne

"Do you see what I see?" I asked Ivan Racz, my companion on a lazy midsummer afternoon.

"American," he answered in a businesslike voice that was not magnetized by the sudden appearance of an absolutely gorgeous blonde at the far end of the swimming pool. He recited her vital statistics in the manner of a tobacco auctioneer.

"Registered as Mrs. Reginald Kelly-Brooks, to throw off the wolves. Actually she's single, real name [as I shall call her] Brenda Kane. New York, Oyster Bay, Palm Beach. Only daughter of the late John Jacob Kane—you know, of Kane razor blades. Heiress in class A-2-x-minus."

"What do you mean class A-2?"

"Not less than two, not more than five million dollars."

"What's the minus for?"

"Money held in trust. Annual income under two hundred thousand dollars."

"I see. What else?"

"Twenty-three years old. Miss Hughes' Classes, Vassar, a year at the Sorbonne. Unmarried, unattached. Measurements," he looked up at her as she was bouncing a crazy-quilt medicine ball, "let me see! 34-20-32, wouldn't you say?"

"I would. She takes my breath away. And from what I can see in the Jantzen, she's an authentic blonde. What is she doing in Budapest?"

"Tourist. Arrived 8:30 a.m. on the Orient Express from Vienna. Checked into Suite 37—the Sunflower Suite—two hundred and fifty pengoes a day. She's chaperoned by Miss Hortense Hathaway, her mother's secretary. Breakfasted at ten —orange juice, one three-minute egg, crackers, coffee with milk, without sugar. No lunch. Expects to stay ten days. No special plans."

"These American girls!" I enthused. "Isn't she the most beautiful young thing you ever saw?"

"I like them older and X-plus."

"What's X-plus?"

"Old gals—widows, divorcees, et cetera. They write their checks without a battery of lawyers breathing down their necks. The young and the beautiful aren't my cup of tea."

"Why?"

"They don't need me."

At that moment, Brenda's medicine ball hit me, portentously, like the apple that fell on Sir Isaac Newton's head.

"I'm so sorry," she said with a winsome smile as she rushed over to retrieve the ball. "I hope I haven't hurt you."

"Not at all, Miss Kane," I said. The smile vanished from her face. She looked at me with unconcealed annoyance, but I went on cheerfully, unaware that I had touched a sensitive nerve. "The pleasure is all mine. I understand you've just arrived in our lovely Budapest. Won't you sit down?"

"No, thank you," she said curtly. She picked up the ball, beckoned to Miss Hathaway, and retreated into the hotel as fast as she could. I saw what Ivan meant. They don't need us.

We were lounging under a shady umbrella at the Gellert's pool, the best place you could be on a summer afternoon if you couldn't afford the Riviera or the North Sea. It was the closest thing to Cannes or Scheveningen that Magyar ingenuity could conjure up by ad libbing an ocean in the heart of Budapest.

A Hungarian engineer invented some contraption that could whip up waves. Then the enterprising manager of the Gellert, Budapest's best hotel, built an enormous swimming pool around the machine, imported authentic salt water and opened up for business as a seashore spa. The pool rolled with better and— when the apparatus ran wild—bigger waves than the Bay of Biscay.

I liked to linger on the windswept shores of this ersatz ocean. It inspired me to wild tales of the sea in the manner of Joseph Conrad. Besides—it also attracted to its artificial beach the most bewitching women of Budapest. Wearing abbreviated bathing suits that antedated the Bikini, the way homemade goose liver preceded canned *pâté de foie gras,* they presented a spectacle of mermaids I am sure no legitimate beach could match.

On this particular sultry afternoon, as I was getting pleasantly high on wine, women and the Gellert's heady air, I had been joined by my friend, Ivan Racz, a very handsome young man whose motive for being on these shores was more naughty than nautical.

Ivan was well known in Budapest as a failure—the failure of his mother, a once enchanting actress of the musical stage named Marika Racz, to persuade the Archduke Salvator that he was Ivan's father. Had she succeeded in this valiant effort to assure a morganatic legitimacy for her son, Ivan would have been a count or something with a trust fund of his own, the usual emolument indiscreet Hapsburgs gave their illegitimate offspring.

However, Marika was turned down flat in a secret session of the Court of Cassation to which she carried her claim. The lawyers of His Royal Highness submitted medical records to show that a delicate injury their client had suffered in the Battle of Sadowa had effectively incapacitated him to sire any children.

Poor Ivan had to grow up penniless. But he also grew up to be fantastically good-looking, a fact he advertised by appearing at the Gellert's poolside in a minimum of concealment, displaying the most breathtaking masculine torso this side of Delphi. And while priceless Greek statuary in Delphi usually has signs cautioning spectators not to touch or handle, Ivan had no lables on him.

Ivan Racz—or Count de Racz, as he would permit himself to be addressed whenever he deemed it expedient to disregard the verdict of the Court of Cassation—was making a living by escorting lonely ladies to the better nocturnal sights of Budapest.

Ivan Racz was a gigolo.

But he wasn't an ordinary gigolo, the fiery-eyed, moustachioed Argentine-type that emotes mechanically at the sound of castanets and marimbas like a war horse when it hears a bugle. Whether or not the venerable archduke had anything to do with his chromosomes, Ivan felt that the blue blood of the Hapsburgs was flowing in his veins. He handled his assignments with superb discretion, giving his clients the impression that he was really Prince Charming. Correspondingly, every old moneybags he happened to have in tow came to feel like Cinderella.

When my fortuitous bumping into Brenda Kane's wayward medicine ball yielded only a rebuff, I gave up the chase and forgot the pretty heiress in class A-2-x-minus. I was, therefore, rather surprised when a few nights later, on a perfunctory tour of the night spots, I discovered her at a cozy table in the

Parisian Grill, holding hands with a young man who looked like a Greek god in bronze. Ivan Racz, of course.

I lingered conspicuously, hoping that they might invite me to their table, but they ignored me just as conspicuously. I had to respect Ivan's professional protocol and I did not want to barge in on him when he was on duty.

Returning home around six in the morning, I prepared to retire for the day when I heard a cab drive up and stop under my window, then saw Ivan climb out. He was still immaculately clad in his working clothes—white dinner jacket with a red carnation, a broad purple cummerbund, and the pair of black pants, his trademark, that a tailor in Madrid had made especially for him. Nothing showed that he had spent the night in pursuit of his profession, not even the faint lipstick smear that sometimes soiled the upper part of his jacket where his clients were wont to lay their heads.

A moment later I heard the doorbell ring and welcomed Ivan into my apartment.

"I have to talk to you," he said.

"What can I give you?" I asked. "Aspirin or a pick-me-up?"

"A shot of helium," he said with a new glint in his eyes. I immediately recognized that this was not the cynical young mercenary I used to know. The change alarmed me.

"Don't bother," he said, "I'm lighter than air anyway."

"Is it Miss Kane?" I asked.

He nodded and said: "I hope you don't mind that I didn't invite you to our table last night. I couldn't very well ask you over after what I'd told Bunny about you."

"Bunny?"

"That's what her father used to call her."

"What did you tell her about me?"

"I told her you were, well, a gigolo. As a matter of fact, I told her you were the most notorious gigolo in town. I had to, don't you see?"

"No, I don't see," I said acidly.

"It was inexcusable," he said, taking the offensive, "that you addressed her as Miss Kane when she came to our table at the Gellert's pool. She was so disturbed that her incognito had been penetrated that she actually told Miss Hathaway to make arrangements to leave Budapest at once."

"I'm sorry. But apparently she's changed her mind."

"Well, I found her with Miss Hathaway in the lobby, sitting like a couple of lost seagulls on a reef. I went over and asked Miss Hathaway if I could talk to her, alone. I told her you were just, well, a gigolo, looking for a client and had made your customary investigation of Brenda because she seemed like a promising newcomer to you. That was how you found out who she really was."

"Incidentally," I asked, "how did you find out?"

"Oh," he said, "I have my methods. I check the hotel registry, examine passports, look people up in the Social Register, Burke's Peerage, the Almanach de Gotha, Who's Who, Dun and Bradstreet. I have my reference library, you see, because in my business I can't leave things to chance. Believe me, a lot of research goes into my work.

"Well, anyway, Miss Hathaway was friendly, especially when I assured her that no gigolo would ever bother Miss Kane again during her stay in Budapest. I'd see to that."

"I see."

"No, you don't," he said. "I'm not interested in her professionally. Well, Miss Hathaway was so grateful that she took me to Bunny—I mean to Miss Kane—and introduced me to her, explaining how I had set myself up as her guardian. She smiled at me and I'm telling you, it gave me a third degree burn, and that was that."

"What?"

"I fell in love with her at first sight."

"Second sight," I said. "At first sight, you told me you

weren't interested in these A-minus types because they didn't know what side your bread is buttered on."

"I'd appreciate it if you'd choose your language with greater care. I'm in love with her and that's what I came here to talk to you about."

"What do you want me to do? Propose on your behalf?"

"No," he said. "I want you to loan me a couple of hundred pengoes because I'm dead broke."

"Aren't you charging her for your services?"

"That's just it," he said. "I couldn't take any money from her if my life depended on it. It's never happened to me before. I'm in love—in l-o-v-e, my dear chap—and, how shall I say, well, it cramps my style."

I saw them in all the summer spots together, as they traveled down the usual lovers' route—from elaborate places like the Grill to more intimate locales like the Kit Kat Klub, and eventually to earthy bistros on the Right Bank in Buda where excellent food and wine are served on coarse tablecloths and gypsy musicians roam about the tables.

I was also receiving periodic visits from Ivan, asking in increasingly desperate terms for additional loans.

"I'm being ruined by this confounded love of mine. A man in my business can't afford to fall in love."

Then one morning he came to me blushing like a schoolboy.

"I hope you don't think I'm a cad," he said, "but you're my only friend and I have to talk it out with you. I'm breaking under the strain."

I offered him another loan.

"No, it isn't only the money part of it. The trouble is, I don't seem to be getting to first base with her. I haven't even kissed her yet, not really, if you know what I mean. She told me she likes me, too, but she can't just fall into my arms because she says she's a Presbyterian and promised her father on his deathbed that she would . . . Oh, hell! I'll go out of my mind if I can't sleep with her."

"How about marrying her?" I said. "That would solve a lot of problems, even if she's in class A-2-x-minus."

"She can't," he said, "not just yet. Some idiotic clause in her dad's will won't let her marry until she's twenty-five. I cannot make any such long-range plans. I want her now, with every fiber in my body, or I'll blow out my brains."

Yet when he returned to me the next morning, Ivan was as jubilant as he had been dejected the day before.

"Everything has changed for the better. She kissed me last night. And she agreed to spend the weekend with me at Lillafured, just the two of us. Imagine—the invigorating air of the mountains, the candlelit dining room, the gypsy violins, champagne, two adjoining rooms! This is the home stretch! Wish me luck!"

I wished him luck and he vanished into the invigorating air of the mountains of Lillafured.

He came to see me Tuesday morning and from the absence of any lipstick smears on his white dinner jacket I could see at once that things had not progressed appreciably in the meantime. He was more dejected than ever.

"You haven't been to Lillafured," I ventured a guess.

"I have."

"She walked out on you."

"Wrong again."

"Then what happened?"

"Nothing," he said. "That's just it! Nothing happened!"

"I think you're just chivalrous, trying to protect a lady's honor. My dear Ivan, after all the things you've told me before, I think you ought to spare me this final suspense."

"I told you, *nothing* happened. We came back to Budapest and that was that. She's leaving tomorrow morning on the

Orient Express. Her mother is waiting for her in Paris. She's a couple of weeks overdue as it is."

I realized he didn't want to be pressed any further, so we let Brenda Kane of New York, Oyster Bay and Palm Beach fade out of our lives.

She left on schedule. Ivan bade her farewell at the railroad station with the most heartbreaking bouquet of red roses I've ever seen. Then he returned to earth. He was again escorting elderly matrons, class B-3-plus or C-1-minus, and once even a dowager who was A-1-plus. He handled them with his usual decorum and tact, and with a newly acquired reserve that was, I thought, the hangover of his stillborn affair with Brenda.

Several months later, I was alone with him one night in the Café New York and found him in a mood for reminiscences. It was, in fact, he who brought her up.

"Do you remember that American girl?" he asked.

"Yes," I said, "and you owe me . . ."

"I know," he said. "I owe you a couple of thousand pengoes."

"Well, yes," I said, "but that wasn't what I meant. You owe me an explanation, my dear Ivan. Remember? The candlelit dining room, the gypsy violins, the invigorating air of the mountains . . ."

"Oh, cut it out!" he said. He became pensive for a moment, then opened up: "As a matter of fact, everything was perfect, much better than I dared to hope. The night we arrived she told me that she had decided to relax her Presbyterian rules and would take a little champagne after all. She had a glass and I could see at once that it was doing the trick."

"What champagne was it?" I asked.

"Veuve Cliquot, 1929," he said.

"No wonder. Go on."

"She became so relaxed—even more beautiful than usual, with a new glow on her face. She had only a single glass but even so when we went upstairs she permitted me to kiss her good night. It was our first *real* kiss. She put so much into it that I tried to follow her into her room. But no dice!"

"What do you expect after a single glass?"

"Right! We had champagne again Saturday night, Pommery, 1931, and she went two glasses. Then champagne again Sunday night. It was Piper-Heidseck, 1927, the best of the lot. She had three glasses downstairs and permitted me to take a bottle upstairs."

"Congratulations," I said.

"We finished the bottle in my room. I knew instinctively, this was it. She was becoming very gay . . . was on the verge of letting her guard down, yet she was still wavering. Now or never, I said, for I was positive that *just one more bottle of champagne* and she would be mine."

"So?"

"There was no more champagne."

"What happened? Was Lillafured out of it?"

"Hell, no," he said. "They had a cellar full. But you see, that was our last night in Lillafured and we were due to motor back to Budapest early the following morning. Before we went upstairs she had paid the bill and what with all that champagne, it was quite a stiff bill. She had to scrape the barrel to pay it."

"She paid the bill?" I echoed, and he said bitterly:

"Yes, of course! And goddam it, it turned out at the critical moment she didn't have enough cash left for one more lousy bottle of champagne."

The House on Depot Street

I COULD NEVER UNDERSTAND WHY SOME PEOPLE HAD TO GO all the way to the South Seas to find a Sadie Thompson when Hungary was so much nearer and had similar attractions galore without any mosquitoes, hot winds and rainy seasons. My own home town was only a small place behind God's back but we had our little Ilonka, for example, and she could have taught Sadie a few new tricks. She caught old Doc Ehmer, of all people, in a pit compared with which the tender trap that Miss Thompson had baited for her missionary was but a mole hole.

The story of Ilonka and our old Doctor goes back some time but it is still fondly remembered in my native patch, where it is rated second only to the case of Anthony and Cleopatra. I was just about twelve years old then, but I knew little Ilonka quite well because I used to frequent the local bagnio where she worked. I hasten to add that I wasn't in the crib to benefit from the libidinous munificence of its seasoned inmates. Although I was a well-grown, normal lad with a fair idea of the facts of life, I was no prodigy. I happened to be the favorite of Doc Ehmer, the District Health Officer, whose chores included regular weekly calls at the brothel to make sure that the girls were as sound as a licensed belle is supposed to be.

Doc Ehmer hoped that one day I also would become a physician and maybe even District Health Officer. In preparation for my future career, he made me read papers on encephalitis lethargica and dropsy, let me handle his scalpels and stethoscopes, and took me along in his buggy on house calls to aid him on odd chores, from carrying his bag to cutting an occasional umbilical cord.

I used to spend my summer vacations entirely with Doc and thus it happened that on Thursday mornings in July and August I accompanied him to the establishment of Madame Vilma.

Although it wasn't as proudly featured as the Teachers College or our War Memorial, Madame Vilma's was definitely one of the landmarks of my home town. It was housed in a long, one-story yellow building behind a tall wall on deserted Depot Street; and though it was—both literally and figuratively—on the wrong side of the railroad tracks, it had a certain class. Even the familiar red lantern over its solid maple gate seemed to be a mark of distinction rather than shame.

As for Vilma, she was a home-grown madame. She started out as a scullery maid in the Count Maray castle on the hill, then became the trusted *femme de chambre* of the Countess. Aside from her regular duties, she, as did most pretty peasant girls, gave practical sex education to two generations of the family on the male side. When she was getting somewhat superannuated to perform such a function for yet another generation of Marays, and announced her decision to shed her amateur status, the Count himself endorsed her application for the necessary franchise. Her other character references included the circuit judge, Doc Ehmer, the president of the District Bank, and the major in charge of our gendarmerie post. Virtually the whole male population of my home town greeted her new venture with profound satisfaction because Vilma was a woman whose vast experience was matched by her utter discretion.

The "salon" she founded was not too big or too lavish, but it was quite cozy with a homelike atmosphere, ideal for men who had grown tired of the atmosphere of their own homes. Most of the time it was stocked with four winsome young ladies. They lived a quiet monastic life behind that discreet wall, playing dominoes, writing letters, knitting garments for their sisters' kids during their long and lonely days, or reading true confession magazines about other peoples' far more complicated romances.

While Doc Ehmer was busy giving the checkups, I sat in the deserted parlor with its piano muted for the day, sipping the cold raspberry soda Madame Vilma always had ready for me. In the beginning I was intrigued by the locale, to be sure, but the novelty wore off and I became blunted to its carnal mysteries. During my morning visits, it was just a spotlessly clean, neat, middle-class abode enveloped in the fragrant aroma of stuffed cabbage cooking for lunch. I don't think my visits at Madame Vilma's left any traumatic residues in me. If anything, they helped me to get a more rounded picture of life at a relatively early age.

Unlike most of Hungary's other institutions, prostitution was astonishingly well organized. While in many countries hypocrisy devises laws for the blood, as Shakespeare put it, compelling hot tempers to leap over cold decrees, Hungary had a set of ordinances on her statute books to guide illicit passion into licit channels. There was a lively white slavery trade in the background of the system with procurers licensed by the police to supply the wares. It enabled the houses to secure new girls every few months and thus provide stimulating variety for their clientele.

From time to time we used to see Madame Vilma, a tall, stout, stern-looking matron, waiting solemnly at the depot for the evening train from Budapest to welcome a new crop of inmates. As soon as the word spread that Madame was at the railroad station, our gay blades flocked to the depot to preview the newcomers from the distance. Carrying battered suitcases and oversized rag dolls in their arms, the girls alighted without ostentation, curtsied to Madame, kissed her hand, then vanished behind the wall.

The town at large had its opportunity to view Madame's young charges each Sunday morning when they paraded down Main Street on their way to church. It was a decorous little procession, chaperoned by Madame, who was an erect monument to impeccable respectability on these parades. The girls dressed in somber black with white lace scarfs covering their heads, holding hands as they walked, their heads held high and looking straight ahead.

I remember when little Ilonka arrived in our town because it was the night of the big blizzard and her train was delayed five hours. Even so, the gay blades kept up their vigil until her train crawled in at last. It came to a reluctant stop in the snow and disgorged the three passengers bound for my home town—three young women consigned to Madame Vilma's. One was a flashy peroxide blonde with rouge smeared over the ravines of her wilted face, trying to make up with *élan vital* for her bygone youth. The other was a jolly little fat girl who giggled all the time and especially when she kissed Madame's gloved hand.

The third was little Ilonka. She was bundled up in a couple of coats and her head was covered by a babushka, leaving little to be seen of little Ilonka. But she moved with a dainty gait and her voice had the tonal quality of silver bells. Somehow the nocturnal audience at the depot sensed at once the birth of a star.

It didn't take long for little Ilonka to make her presence felt even in circles that did not normally patronize Madame's establishment. The bachelors who frequented it soon began to speak knowingly and approvingly of her. The starry-eyed young pharmacist clerk, who wrote lyric poetry in secret, embarked on a project that had for its aim the saving of little Ilonka's soul. But her appeal wasn't confined to bachelors. The manager of the flax factory, for instance, was rumored to have told his wife, a lazy, double-chinned woman who had grown stale in the safe haven of wedlock:

"Goddamit, Klari, why can't you be a little like little Ilonka?" To which the lady answered with a question of her own:

"Just how do you know so well how little Ilonka is?"

In due course, little Ilonka became responsible for a sudden invigoration of marital passion in our town as sedate wives, fearful of that competition on Depot Street, put a little more pep into their billings and cooings.

According to the version I was able to piece together when I reached more adult years, nobody could define exactly the secret of little Ilonka's lure, except that she was what the young pharmacist called "so different." A simple girl like the rest of Madame's, she was more delicate than the others, built with childlike fragility. She had a round face, artlessness shining in her big brown eyes, which, however, strange as it may seem, also reflected some impish guile and pristine sophistication. She was friendly and cheerful but skittish with men, her professional levity tempered by coy reserve. Her delicate air and little ladylike *maintien* won for her the unstinted approbation of such connoisseurs as the math teacher of the high school and traveling salesmen from Budapest.

Though Madame's established policy was to infuse fresh

blood into her establishment as often as possible, Ilonka became a permanent fixture. Her clientele never tired of this innocent-looking little strumpet with the comportment of a *grande demoiselle* to whom the sordid pleasures of the house seemed to be a secret game, a furtive intermezzo rather than a tedious chore.

Virtually the only man in town—aside, of course, from the monsignor—who seemed to remain unaffected by little Ilonka's mysterious lure was Doc Ehmer. He was a dedicated country doctor wrapped up in his calling, probably because he had nothing else in life to be wrapped up in. He was a jaunty little man in his late fifties, a genial and happy-go-lucky fellow who looked at the world through pink glasses. He wasn't a very competent physician—his staple remedy for any ailment was a secret formula that, on closer scrutiny, turned out to be Epsom salts—but he was a wise man with a great deal of common sense. He made himself useful in our town far beyond his duties as District Health Officer.

All his ebullient good cheer abruptly ended when he returned home to his dehydrated wife, who had no compassion for Doc's calling or understanding of his love of life. Quite a bit taller than her stocky husband, she was a stern-visaged, extremely thin woman who looked much older than her forty years. If she had any blood in her veins, it wasn't readily evident. To complicate things, the household also included a gangling teen-age son from Mrs. Ehmer's first marriage. His sole function seemed to be to echo his mother's laments about the distinct comedown the Doc represented after her first husband, of blessed memory.

Spring came and then the summer was upon us, renewing my medical season when I made the rounds with Doc and dropped in at Madame Vilma's, where nothing ever seemed to change except the girls. Ilonka was still in residence and by then she was accepted in town as a regular. Each Thursday morning, Doc Ehmer went through the checkups in his usual brisk manner, lightening the humdrum gynecological routine with wisecracks and little compliments.

I did not notice then, but later I recalled, that Doc was devoting increasing attention to the state of Ilonka's health, or at least so it seemed, because he kept spending far more time with her than with the others. In the buggy, after we left the house on Depot Street, he would make an occasional off-hand remark in which Ilonka figured with growing prominence. "That little Ilonka," he once murmured to himself, "she's quite a gal!" And another time in what promised to become a longer dissertation, he mused:

"Strange how different some of these girls can be. Take little Ilonka, for example." But he dropped the subject abruptly and I never found out what made Ilonka so different. In the meantime she had become so popular that one could see her only by appointment, as with Viki Sass, the barber in the District Bank building. She was such a celebrated attraction that a tryst with her became the routine of male visitors bent on doing the town.

In August, I think it was, on one of our Thursday mornings, Doc showed up in the double-breasted blue serge suit he normally wore only on Sundays or when called to the castle to give Epsom salts to one or another of the Marays. Aside from his regular bag he also put a big valise into the buggy, then off we went, first to see old Geszti, whose asthma was giving him trouble in the hot weather, and then to Madame Vilma's.

Doc took care of the three other girls quickly, then spent an unusually long time with little Ilonka. When he returned to the parlor at last where Madame Vilma was waiting for the clean bill of health, he was flushed and more serious than ever.

"Anything wrong, Doc?" Madame asked apprehensively.

"Yes," Doc said gravely. "Little Ilonka."

Madame blew up. "I knew it'd happen one of these days," she sputtered. "All that out-of-town riffraff she's seeing! I bet it was that four-flushing mechanic, the fellow who came from Budapest to fix up the truck of the flax factory."

"No, it isn't that," Doc Ehmer said quietly. "I'm afraid Ilonka has pulmonary phthisis."

Madame was perplexed. Whatever it was, it didn't sound like any of the occupational ills Doc Ehmer would find once in a while despite the meticulous hygiene Madame Vilma insisted upon in the conduct of her business.

"What's that, Doc?" she asked suspiciously. "Something like the dose or maybe, God forbid, sy . . . ?"

"Oh, no," Doc cut her short. "It isn't like one of the things you know. It's like TB, a wasting disease of the lungs. It's a very serious ailment, Vilma."

"My God," Madame wailed and crossed herself. "Could she maybe even die from it?"

"I'm afraid she could, under certain circumstances," Doc said. "There is this progressive emaciation, for instance, that goes with pulmonary phthisis, and a continuous destruction of the tissues. But she can still be saved, I believe, provided . . ."

"Provided what, Doc?" Vilma asked anxiously.

"Provided we get her to the hospital at once."

"What do you want me to do?"

"There is nothing you can do, Vilma," Doc said as he looked at his watch. "It's now just twelve fifteen. We can easily make the one o'clock train to Kaposvar." It was the county seat, with the nearest hospital. "I told Ilonka to pack her things because I'm going to take her to Kaposvar myself."

"Oh, Doc Ehmer," Madame Vilma cried, "it's nice of you but you shouldn't go to so much trouble."

"No trouble," Doc murmured and drew a deep puff on his pipe. "No trouble at all, I assure you."

They left on the one o'clock train, Ilonka looking a little too radiant for someone suffering from pulmonary phthisis and the Doc far too pale and feeble for a presumably healthy District Health Officer. I stood on the platform watching them leave and wondered why the old Doc had put so much feeling into the embrace with which he bid me good-by. As the train began to pull out, he opened the window and called out to me:

"Remember me, son, always remember me, no matter what! And by the way, tell my wife I won't be home for dinner."

When he wasn't back home for next day's lunch either, Mrs. Ehmer called the hospital in Kaposvar to find out what was keeping her husband. She was told they hadn't seen the Doc and hadn't a patient named Ilonka suffering from pulmonary phthisis.

The first we heard from them was five years later when Madame Vilma received a picture postcard from a place called Nukualofa or something, showing a group of pretty young girls dancing on a beach under some palm trees, their firm breasts bared to the trade winds.

It was from little Ilonka and it read:

"Dear Madame Vilma. I hope this will find you in the best of health. Thank God, I am in the best of health myself and happy. Kindest regards, Little Ilonka. P.S. Doc Ehmer sends his regards. He is also in the best of health and very happy."

When she couldn't find Nukualofa on the map of Hungary, Madame Vilma took the postcard to Jeno Simon, the geography teacher at the high school; and Simon told her that it was very much farther than Kaposvar, farther even than Budapest. It was, he said with his customary erudition, the capital of an island called Tonga in the South Pacific where the reefs were gray and the shore was steep, and the winds blew soft and sweet.

"It's sometimes also called the Friendly Island," Simon added, and Madame Vilma murmured pensively:

"I thought so."

 *Uncle Gyula*

'TWAS THE NIGHT BEFORE YOU KNOW WHAT IN MY LITTLE home town of Csurgo and the air was filled with great expectations, except one—we didn't expect Uncle Gyula home for Christmas. This was, of course, the most joyous time of the year and the family overflowed with good will to men, to all men except my Uncle Gyula. He stood for none of the things Christmas symbolized and created some commotion when he suddenly burst into our Yuletide bliss.

To say he burst in is somewhat overstating it. He, rather, slid silently in just as we were sitting down to our festive dinner. My grandfather was poised to carve the goose when Rozika, our pretty upstairs maid, rushed into the dining room and announced:

"Master Gyula is outside in a sled. He says he needs a hundred forint in cash before he can come in."

A hundred forint was a small fortune in those days, but more intrigued than angered, my grandfather took the cash from the safe and went outside to see why his prodigal son had to be ransomed. In the mellow twilight of this Christmas eve, he found my uncle in the back seat of an open sled, wrapped in a huge Siberian overcoat and an assortment of wool blankets embroidered with the words "Hotel Ritz."

"What is the meaning of this?" my grandfather asked sternly, and Uncle Gyula said: "I'll explain everything, Father, but first give the money to the driver or else he won't let me make land. I've been on the road since the day before yesterday and I'm frozen stiff in this confounded conveyance." His voice sounded distant and weak, muffled as it was by an enormous fur cap pulled down over his face.

Up front in the sled sat the Santa Claus who had brought him, a little wizened old man almost lost in a huge quilted coat, his patriarchal beard solidified in a glistening array of icicles. He peered over a pair of icebound spectacles with one suspicious eye on my uncle and the other on his two skinny horses, which stood stolidly in the snow, enveloped in the vapor of their perspiration.

Santa turned out to be Mr. Samuel Horowitz, a veteran cabbie from Budapest. Sam's presence, almost two hundred kilometers from his regular stand in front of the Ritz Hotel, was an event without precedent and an indication of an *in extremis* situation. Budapest cabbies in general were the most hardboiled couriers known to transportation and Sam, in particular, was the hardest. Moreover, this was 1912, when Hungarian roads were not yet fit for long-distance commuting. But by promising Sam the royal reward of a hundred forint, my Uncle Gyula succeeded in bamboozling him into making the icy trip and even to advance the incidental expenses of the journey.

Uncle Gyula's persuasive mastery stemmed from a one-exit situation. He had the sudden filial urge to contact my grandfather in a matter of some delicacy but had no funds for the railroad trip or for any form of transportation where the fare had to be paid in advance.

I was overwhelmed by my uncle's arrival in the grand style of St. Nicholas. He was my favorite uncle, whose comings always thrilled me because he brought expensive off-beat gifts for me and turned my drab little life in the country into brief periods of enchantment. I was then six years old and the only member of the family he managed to enchant. Everybody else viewed his arrivals as unmitigated misfortunes. He was the black sheep and his homecoming gifts to them consisted of his troubles.

This time his trouble was most appropriate for the season. It involved turkeys, or rather a sudden shortage of them in England, of all places, for which His Majesty's Government held my uncle responsible. It seems he had sold several train-loads of the popular birds to wholesalers in London and then neglected their delivery. This created an acute culinary crisis in England (where Hungarian turkeys used to be most popular) and brought Scotland Yard into the picture. Uncle Gyula, I am embarrassed to say, had pocketed substantial advances. The Yard duly apprised the police of Budapest, and my uncle took Sam for a sleigh ride when he heard Detective Kallay of the Fraud and Forgery Squad asking for him at the desk of the Hotel Ritz, where he was living in style on the last vestiges of his advances.

By looking at my Uncle Gyula, you would never have thought him capable of depriving those nice Britons of their favorite Christmas treat. In actual fact, he was extremely fond of England and tried his best to look like an Englishman, to the point of going out into the noonday sun with a rolled-up umbrella. When he wasn't wearing a Siberian overcoat and fur cap, he was an attractive young man with a trim figure, trustful eyes and a perennial friendly smile on his well-shaped lips. His natural good looks were enhanced by his pleasant personality. He was suave and polite, speaking in a low, soft voice that by itself elicited implicit faith. He dressed with the quiet elegance of Bond Street, and carried the usual paraphernalia of the accomplished dandy—soft mohair spats, ebony cane with a silver head, gold cigarette case, emerald tie pin, a single brilliant on his right pinky and a huge signet ring on his left middle finger displaying what he claimed, with considerable genealogical license, was the family coat of arms. He managed to be so well decked out by charging everything to my grandfather's accounts or by somehow eliciting credit.

Uncle Gyula needed this finery to succeed in his chosen profession. We in the family referred to him as a financier, but in actual fact he was a general practitioner of the artful dodge. A man of considerable ingenuity, he practiced his trade along original lines, specializing in a single and rare form of flimflammery. He was what he himself called a linguist, although he spoke only his native Hungarian; but that with ingratiating fluency.

Among the many problems that vex them as a nation, their language represents a perplexing dilemma to most Hungarians. Every person belongs to what is called a speech community and Hungarians are, of course, no exceptions, but the speech community to which they belong is an exceptionally restricted one. Preposterous though it may seem to claim that Zsa Zsa Gabor might have anything in common with a round-faced, blubber-scented Eskimo woman from a primitive Asian tribe called Ostyaks, the fact is she has—the language. Hungarian belongs to the Ugric group of the Finno-Ugric family of languages, which is spoken, aside from Hungarians, only by some thirty thousand Ostyaks and Voguls in a place called Khanti-Mansi in a godforsaken part of northern Siberia.

Speaking a tongue that is tantamount to a lingua obscura, Hungarians are enamoured with foreign languages and often become prolific in several of them. My Uncle Gyula was

simply infatuated with the sound of foreign tongues but, unlike most Hungarians, he had absolutely no talent for them
and was far too indolent to learn any the hard way. But his
inability to acquire any of those tantalizing foreign tongues
did not faze him. He could never learn to play the viola pomposa either, yet he often claimed he was a virtuoso of that
old instrument. It was a rather safe pretense because rare was
the house he visited that had a viola pomposa handy.

In due course, Uncle Gyula blossomed out as a linguist *in
petto,* so to speak. In unusually jaunty moments he would
claim he spoke forty-three languages with consummate fluency.
They were unusually rare and difficult tongues, such as: Mish-
mi, Kohistani and Limbu, or Rhaeto-Romanic and Dyak, in
which nobody in Budapest could challenge him to a conversation. After a while he actually persuaded himself that he
was, indeed, an extraordinary linguist and once even applied
at the Peter Pazmany University for a job as instructor of
Sanskrit. Unfortunately, the University had several scholars
who were fluent in that classic tongue and one of them was
delegated by the dean to test my uncle's qualifications. When
he asked Gyula to translate a passage from the *Sakuntala,* he
solved the problem with his customary *sang-froid* by asking:

"What language is this, Professor?"

"Sanskrit, of course."

"Oh," my uncle said with a disarming smile, "I'm so sorry.
It's my fault. I thought you were looking for someone with
a knowledge of Sans*krott,* a rare dialect, as you undoubtedly
know, in the Yod-Tinctura sub-family, spoken only by a handful of natives in Lower Polynesia."

While he failed to land the job at the University, Uncle
Gyula did succeed in getting two excellent employments as
a linguist, enabling him to live quite well for years.

He landed the first job by answering an ad in the *Pesti
Hirlap* in which a group of Hungarian big game hunters sought

the services of a man fluent in Swahili to serve as their interpreter on a safari in darkest Africa. My uncle applied, gave a breathtaking demonstration of his fluency in Swahili (which, he said, he had learned as the child of a missionary in Zanzibar) and was hired because nobody in the group, of course, knew even a word of the language.

My uncle went on the safari and acquitted himself with flying colors by addressing the good-natured natives in fluent double-talk he described as "argotic pig Swahili." Combining expressive gestures with his gibberish and through the meaningful intonation of his self-made words, he somehow managed to make himself understood. Everything went well until one day he misunderstood a native and embroiled the hunters in the vast Bantu swamps in hot pursuit of a herd of rhinos. My uncle was saved from the consequences of this misunderstanding by a sudden attack of amnesia.

His other major linquistic venture was just as exciting but far less macabre in its outcome. Again it was a classified ad in the *Pesti Hirlap* that brought him the job on which he was to subsist rather well for two whole years. The ad sought a French instructor for a high school boy on a full-time basis, offering board and lodgings, and a salary of fifty forints a month. Uncle Gyula presented himself as a former associate professor of Romance languages at the Sorbonne. The boy he was to instruct was the elder son of an immensely wealthy wholesale butcher who was anxious to give his offspring the education he himself had missed.

Uncle Gyula moved into the cozy room the wholesale butcher provided for him, lived well in a household whose cuisine benefited vastly from the father's business, had a highly satisfactory affair with the pretty Austrian governess of the younger son, and spent two hours every afternoon teaching French. He proved a patient and conscientious teacher, hammering all the intricacies of Gallic grammar into his pupil's somewhat thick head and making him learn by heart fifteen words each day from a glossary he himself had prepared, until the boy could converse fluently with his teacher in what was supposed to be Voltaire's tongue.

His pleasant sinecure terminated when the youth was sent to France to study at the famed University of Grenoble. The boy was quite dull-witted, to be sure, but even so he was nonplussed when nobody in Grenoble could comprehend his French and when, in turn, they spoke a rather strange gibberish that he could not understand.

Undaunted, Uncle Gyula answered yet another ad in the *Pesti Hirlap,* the one that was to lead eventually to his frantic turkey trot seeking my grandfather's aid during that momentous Christmas of 1912. The ad was placed by a big export firm specializing in turkeys, seeking someone to handle its correspondence with customers in England, where, as we have noted, Hungarian turkeys were exceptionally popular. Posing as the illegitimate son of Lord Loganberry who had migrated to Budapest when his poor mother had to take a job with the Count Paloczys as an English governess, Uncle Gyula got the job. Somehow or other he even managed to survive in it, producing English letters culled word by word from Dr. Arthur Yolland's two-volume Hungarian-English dictionary. Thus, for instance, he once wrote the following letter, which was preserved by my humorous grandfather as a bit of family folklore:

"On big regret inform you that have no fashion in you deliver the 3,000 turkey which you have heart order flowing snow in sixth in letter in."

In proper translation, the letter should have read more or less: "We greatly regret to inform you that we are unable to deliver the 3,000 turkeys you ordered in your esteemed letter of the sixth of this month."

In stringing his dictionary-picked words together like beads,

Uncle Gyula had overlooked the possibility of double meanings, such as *szivesek,* which may be translated either as "pleased" or "heart," and *ho,* which may mean either "snow" or "month."

Even so, there was never any objection to his English letters. On his own volition, he finally resigned in righteous indignation when his boss objected to a letter he had written in Hungarian. He stayed just long enough to write one more masterpiece on the firm's letterhead: a glowing recommendation of himself, attesting that he had been an executive of the company in charge of foreign sales for seven years. The recommendation also cited him as a graduate veterinarian specializing in the diseases of the *Meleagris gallopovo,* the domesticated turkey, and one of the leading turkey-breeders of Central Europe.

Using the document, he set himself up in business and sold turkeys by the thousands to the customers of his former firm. They flocked to him because his prices were substantially lower and his terms more accommodating, except that he required twenty per cent in advance.

As a result, Uncle Gyula received a Christmas present from my grandfather after all. Our grand old man bailed him out again, but that was the last time he was prepared to take Uncle Gyula off the hook.

"I'm sending you to the United States of America," grandfather told him. It was the customary solution of the problem.

"But what am I going to do in America?" my uncle protested in panic.

"Sell matches," grandfather replied ironically, without weighing the potential implications of his words.

My uncle made the trip in style, dining at the captain's table and enjoying the favors of several stage-struck young ladies to whom he had introduced himself as the director of the Ballet of Monte Carlo. But no sooner was he settled in New York than we received a cable from him.

"Urgently need two hundred dollars," he wired, "to buy matches."

Impressed and pleased that my uncle had turned irony to profit, my grandfather sent him the money. Then came another plea: "Please cable five hundred dollars, must buy cigarettes."

This was a puzzler, if only because Uncle Gyula did not smoke. My grandfather cabled back: "Please explain."

Gyula's answer arrived promptly and it gave us an insight into the manners and mores in America.

"Matches are given away free with purchase of cigarettes," he wrote. "Need cigarettes to get rid of my matches."

Shavers of
the Wind

HUNGARIAN FOR EARNING MONEY IS *penzt keresni,* WHICH in literal translation means searching for or seeking money, and the phrase went far to show that the filthy lucre didn't grow on trees in the old days in my native land. Yet it didn't take much to be a millionaire in Budapest, as you could have gathered from a brief exchange I once had with my friend Zoltan Baroti after bumping into Miksa Pauncz on the Ring. Pauncz was a memorial real estate man, as he called himself, selling cemetery plots, and doing rather well at it.

"Now there's a millionaire for you," Zoltan said with a touch of envy as he looked admiringly after Miksa.

"A millionaire?" I replied. "He's lucky if he has ten thousand pengoes!"

"Well?" Zoltan said. "Isn't that enough?"

Although under their current Communist regime money has lost much of its old allure, Hungarians still cherish fond memories of it and have a warm spot in their memories for a certain Morton Jellinek, whom they regard as the greatest financial wizard Hungary produced in this century. Morton became a millionaire by absconding with a hundred thousand dollars. What made him such a wizard was that he stole it from the police.

Jellinek originally was a stockbroker but when he couldn't eke out a living at that he switched to foreign-exchange negotiations, a forbidden and, therefore, more promising field. Hungary, at that time, had a strict currency law prohibiting all private trading in foreign money. This led to a flourishing black market, which was frequently raided by the detectives of a special branch of the Budapest police called the Valuta Squad.

In costly fashion, Jellinek learned the hazards and financial drawbacks of the trade. In the end, the fox decided to run with the hounds. He set himself up as an informer, steering the police to clandestine valuta transactions on a commission basis. After a string of minor coups that yielded only modest commissions, he came to Inspector Fuezessy, head of the Valuta Squad, one day with a prime prospect.

"Inspector," he said breathlessly, "I've just come upon a multimillion-dollar syndicate. Big time, you understand—strictly American currency."

"Who are they and where do they operate?" the Inspector asked with a blunt naïveté characteristic of police officers.

"Ah," said Morton wryly, "it isn't as simple as just names and places. We have to trap these people *in flagrante*, else how do you expect to lay your hands on the valuta and get evidence for a conviction?"

"True, true. And I can see you have a plan," said the great sleuth.

"I do," Jellinek enthused. "We could break the backbone of the whole syndicate and confiscate their entire working capital. All you have to do is set me up so I can trap them in a big deal."

"How?" the Inspector asked.

"Through my line to the syndicate I'd offer it a hundred-thousand-dollar transaction—do you get the idea?"

"No, I don't," Fuezessy confessed. "Go on."

"Well, just when I'm consummating the deal—hand over the hundred thousand, that is, and getting something like two million pengoes in return—you'll spring the trap. You'll be able to pick up the top men in the syndicate together with their money."

"Terrific!" the Inspector exclaimed. "Go ahead, Jellinek, but keep us posted, old man."

"Yes, sir," Morton said, "but . . ."

"But what?" the Inspector asked.

"The bait—the hundred thousand dollars . . ."

"Oh," the Inspector sighed. "Of course, that's a hitch. Well, there goes another good opportunity."

"Not necessarily," Morton said eagerly. "I know somebody who could raise the hundred thousand."

"Who?"

"You."

"Me?!" Fuezessy managed to convey shock and incredulity at the same time.

"I don't mean you personally, Inspector," Jellinek reassured him. "I mean the police. You could borrow the dollars from the National Bank, for a few hours, if you explained you needed them as a bait."

Fuezessy went whole hog for the deal. He arranged the short-term loan of $100,000 in twenty-dollar bills. Jellinek then set up the deal for the following Wednesday at 3 p.m., at the Credit Bank, Hungary's foremost financial institution.

Carrying the dollars in a suitcase, Jellinek went to the rendezvous, followed surreptitiously by Fuezessy and his detectives. According to plan, they trailed Morton to the third floor of the big bank building and took up their battle stations in the corridor. Jellinek marched directly to one of the doors lining the corridor and entered.

Fuezessy and the detectives waited the thirty minutes Jellinek had estimated he would require to set up the trap, and then broke through the door he had entered.

There was no room and, of course, no Jellinek.

The door led to a back staircase by which Jellinek had made his escape with the suitcase full of twenty-dollar bills from the National Bank. He was never found and the police of Budapest are still trying to puzzle out how he managed to vanish without a trace and be off for Argentina, all apparently within the half hour the detectives waited outside the blind door.

Morton Jellinek's cunning coup earned for him widespread admiration in Hungary, and not merely because he had made a fool of the valuta cops. His deed was acclaimed as a sporting feat. In Hungary such lucrative wars of wits were highly regarded and the warriors considered members of a quasi-legitimate enterprise—legitimate, that is, up to the split second of getting caught.

Every nation has its characteristic national crime at which it excels. In Germany it used to be genocide. In France it is forgery. Britons are the world's best cat burglars, and Latins outdo all as jewel thieves. Hungary's favorite crime was what Americans, with misplaced solemnity, call the confidence game.

To be sure, con-manship is neither exclusive nor indigenous to Hungarians. It is practiced vigorously the world over and in some countries with far greater skill than in Hungary. This is reflected in the different colorful names by which con-men are called in the various countries. The British call them "horse copers." The Spanish refer to them as *picaros,* after a celebrated old rogue. The French have the act but no specific name for its practitioners. The Germans say they are *Hochstapler,* or high pilers.

In Hungary, con-men are called *szelhamosok,* which means "shavers of the wind." As the subtle poesy of the phrase indicates, Hungarians practice con-manship not as mundane larceny but rather as a romantic *divertissement.* Virtually the whole nation plays the game in one form or another, so that wind-shaving could be called Hungary's national pastime, like baseball in the United States or adultery in France.

It cuts across all strata of Hungary's social structure. There are self-made con-men who con their way into the big time from humble beginnings, like Menyus Horvath, a gypsy boy who shook down the Credit Lyonnais, the great French bank, to the tune of a million dollars. At the other end are the gentlemen con-men, who do it *pour l'art,* actually oblivious to the fact that they're doing it at all. During the closing stage of World War II, General Sandor Voros, chief of staff of the Hungarian Army, held a melancholy conference with his German opposite number, General Heinz Guderian, and so impressed the German with his apparent loyalty to their common cause that Guderian gave him a de luxe Mercedes staff car as a parting gift. Voros rode off in it and drove straight to Red Army headquarters to surrender the Hungarian Army to the Russians.

In their blissful philosophy, Hungarians perceive no incompatibility between honor and turpitude. A case in point is that of a debonair Hungarian refugee arrested for conning army goods from an American depot in Bavaria and selling them at fantastic prices on the black market. Americans could cope with escapees from behind the Iron Curtain, except when dealing with Czechs and Hungarians—the Czechs because they are sullen and taciturn, the Hungarians because they are outgoing and loquacious. In this particular case, the Hungarian responded to interrogation with bubbly eloquence, exasperating the American captain in charge with a string of contradictory "confessions," the gist of which was, "I just happened to be standing there, waiting for a streetcar."

In the end, the American blew his top and began yelling at the Hungarian, who calmly admonished him: "You don't have to get excited, captain. We can handle this like gentlemen."

There is, I think, a clinical explanation for this attitude, deeply rooted in the Hungarian national character. By its very nature, con-manship presupposes a paranoid personality. It is a psychosis consisting of delusion and deception. But contrary to most peoples, who regard paranoia as a mental disorder, Hungarians consider it a normal state of mind and enjoy it hugely. They revel in delusions and regard their hallucinations as the voices of experience. When delusions are put to practical use, you get the Hungarian brand of the con game.

Of course, the confidence game has its economic aspects everywhere in the world, but only in Hungary is it the cornerstone of a country's entire national economy. According to my friend Rudi Loewinger, the distinguished Hungarian economist, it is at least partly responsible for a Hungarian version of prosperity.

"Look how it works," Rudi explained. "Let's assume you need a winter coat, one of those chichi things made of the best English fabric with a cozy mouton lining and an elegant astrakhan fur collar that sells for a couple of thousand pengoes. Let's further assume you succeed in conning Samu Wertheimer the clothier into giving it to you on credit. You might not realize it, but by walking out with that exquisite coat you've made the economy of Hungary hum merrily."

"I did?" I asked, because I am not too good an economist.

"Of course," Rudi said. "You gave business to Wertheimer,

didn't you? In turn, he gave business to his wholesaler, to the firm that imported the fabric from England, to the Royal Hungarian Railroads, which transported it, to the furrier, to a bunch of tailors, and so on, even aside from giving work to Wertheimer's bookkeeper, who had to charge the coat in the books. Then, of course, you fail to pay for the winter coat."

"I don't," I said, mechanically.

"By not paying for the coat," he went on implacably, "you give employment to bill collectors, paper manufacturers, printers, the Royal Hungarian Postal Administration, et cetera. In the end you're sued and thereby assure work for lawyers, judges, process servers and all the rest, until you give work to the bailiff who picks up the unpaid winter coat. But by that time, this represents no hardship on you because the summer has rolled around and you'd be ridiculous wearing a coat with an astrakhan collar in the heat wave. But soon it's winter again and you need another coat."

"Naturally," I said. "After all, I can't be expected to go without a warm coat in that cold."

"You see?" Rudi said, pleased that I was catching on. "So this time you go to Neumann the clothier and con him into giving you a fine cashmere thing on credit and though it might not have a mouton lining and an astrakhan collar, it'll start the cycle from scratch."

Thus Hungary's well-dressed wind-shavers were among the major sources of Hungarian prosperity. The system permeated the entire economy of the country and affected all its branches. I once heard a prominent furniture dealer say: "In my business I can afford to live rather well, spend a few winter weeks in Davos and the summer at Lake Balaton, send my boy to Oxford and my daughter to the best finishing school in Switzerland. The only thing I can't afford is to pay my wholesalers."

That wind-shaving had a quasi-official status in Hungary became abundantly clear in 1920, when the government itself appeared mysteriously in the sinister background of one of history's most ambitious confidence operations. Dismembered and humiliated by the peace treaty after World War I, Hungary held France responsible for the harsh punishment she received for losing the war. The country was encircled by France's poor relatives in Central Europe, the so-called Little Entente of parvenu countries, Czechoslovakia, Rumania and Yugoslavia. This gave rise to a venomous Bad Neighbor Policy, but Hungary was far too weak to remedy the situation by war.

If she had no recourse to a clash of arms, she could still wage a war of wits. A plot was hatched to shake the foundations of the Little Entente countries by dealing France, their sponsor, a mortal blow. But how? Simple! A major power like France stood or fell on the stability of its currency. If only the franc could be undermined, France would be driven into a financial crisis and take the Little Entente with her into the abyss.

Extremists in the Hungarian government decided to mount a frontal attack on the franc by dumping enormous quantities on the international money market, thus creating a depression from which France would never recover. As in the case of Jellinek, there was but one hitch—where to get the francs. In this case, the Hungarian National Bank had virtually none. Such minor handicaps never discourage Hungarians. If they had no francs to dump, they would make them and dump anyway. In the deepest secrecy, the Hungarian government became a counterfeiter. Millions of francs were surreptitiously printed from meticulously copied plates in the government's own Royal Hungarian Cartographic Institute, with excellent results.

Off the presses of the Institute (which also printed Hungary's own money) came crisp franc notes, so well faked that not even Monsieur le Président of the Banque de France could distinguish them from the genuine articles. In no time, Hungary had all the francs needed to stage its financial raid.

The operation was plotted inside VK-II, the Intelligence branch of the Hungarian General Staff. Officers of the branch were assigned the intricate job of dumping the counterfeit francs on the international market. The plan was to send scores of officers to the various capitals of the world with millions of francs.

Captain Viktor de Gyarmathy, a suave Intelligence officer whose shifty eyes and swarthy complexion made him look like a Levantine horse coper, was picked to do the dumping in the Netherlands. He arrived in Amsterdam with a suitcase full of francs. Courtesy of the Royal Hungarian Cartographic Institute, the francs were of excellent make, but the suitcase was not. When Captain de Gyarmathy lugged it through the lobby of his hotel in Amsterdam, the suitcase sprang open. The possession of a valise full of francs by a shifty-eyed swarthy stranger who looked like a Levantine horse coper attracted attention and the Dutch police made an investigation. The owner of the suitcase was exposed as an officer of the Hungarian General Staff, and then Gyarmathy himself divulged the plot.

Embarrassed by the premature explosion of the plot, the Hungarian government disclaimed complicity in it and farcically arrested a few members of the inner ring. However, deeming the act a patriotic deed rather than a garden variety crime, the honorable judges of Hungary couldn't find any punishment to fit it. When the excitement died down, as such excitements usually do, the men involved in the bizarre venture were awarded a Meritorious Service Medal.

Most of the time, it should be stated, con-manship flourished as private enterprise in Hungary. If Jellinek specialized in the police, one of his great predecessors, a delightful wind-shaver named Ignacz Strassnoff, had as his target the Roman Catholic hierarchy. His off-beat choice had several advantages. For one thing, he could be fairly certain that the ecclesiastical authorities he bilked would never prosecute him. The publicity would have been embarrassing. For another, it was an exclusive field.

Strassnoff was a distinguished-looking, tall gentleman, groomed with conservative elegance. Although he wasn't even a Catholic, he posed as the nephew of the Archbishop of Eger and claimed he was the chief fiscal agent of the Church. In that capacity he would pounce upon one diocese after another to audit their books. Invariably he would uncover shortages. Producing authentic-looking credentials in ornate Latin giving him complete authority in such cases, he would dismiss the guilty bishops and order them to retire to nearby monasteries to contemplate in seclusion the seriousness of their malfeasance.

Then, at the psychological moment, he would broadly hint that he was a reasonable man. The bishops understood the hint. He thus shook down one bishop after another, if only because each one, embarrassed by shortages that, after all, could have existed, kept the secret of the auditor's visit strictly to himself.

Strassnoff's work of art was his coup at Zagreb. He arrived unannounced as usual to audit the books of the Croatian diocese, spent a week poring over the ledgers, then sent word to the Bishop that he had to see him at his earliest inconvenience. When he was closeted with the Bishop, Strassnoff said ominously:

"I'm afraid I've bad news for you, Most Reverend Sir."

"Is it something you found in the books?" the Bishop asked.

"No, Most Reverend Bishop. It is something I did *not* find in the books. It pains me to say that a very substantial sum is conspicuous by its absence in the sacred exchequer of Your Excellency's diocese."

The news was a real shocker but it seemed that Strassnoff had found his match at last. The Bishop of Zagreb refused to accept the audit as accurate and then indignantly spurned Strassnoff's suggestion that he buy himself out of the mess.

The rebuff neither rattled nor fazed Strassnoff. If anything, it made him even more determined to carry the thing to its illogical conclusion.

"I'm sorry, Most Reverend Sir," he told the Bishop in an injured tone, "but Your Excellency leaves me no alternative." He then formally dethroned the Bishop and sent him to do penance in the monastery at Karlovac. With the Bishop out of the way, Strassnoff pulled the most fantastic spoof of his career. He auctioned off the Bishopric among the monsignori of Zagreb and appointed the highest bidder to the vacant seat.

The daring coup came out, of course, but by the time the *status quo ante* was restored in Zagreb, Strassnoff was safely in Paris. He retired there in comfort on the yield of his dazzling career as an ecumenical fiscal agent.

The uncrowned king of con-men in all the world was a Hungarian impostor, a character unfavorably known as Ignatius (after St. Ignatius of Antioch) Timothy (after the companion of St. Paul) Trebitsch (after his father) Lincoln (after Abe). He was the only foreigner ever to be elected a member of the British Parliament and the only Hungarian ever to become the abbot of a Buddhist monastic order. In his person, con-manship reached its pinnacle. It transcended by far its usual confines of larceny, and became a vast international maneuver in the course of which this remarkable man once tried to sink the British fleet singlehanded.

The son of a well-to-do lumber merchant at Paks, a small Hungarian city on the Danube, young Isaac Trebitsch (as he was actually named) was slated for the rabbinate. But he quarreled with his devout father, left Hungary in a huff, and went to England, where he became a Lutheran. Later he migrated to Canada to work with a Presbyterian mission to the Jews. When the mission was absorbed in the Church of England, he became an Anglican.

Upon his return to England, the intrepid missionary was duly ordained and appointed curate at the parish of Appledore in Kent by the Archbishop of Canterbury, who developed a paternal interest in this eager-beaver young convert. But his oratory in a thick Hungarian accent did not appeal to his Kentish parishioners, so Lincoln left Appledore in disgust, turned his back on the Church of England, and went back to London to become a journalist. At some stage of his journalistic career, he met the philanthropist Seebohm Rowntree, a multimillionaire manufacturer who was the moving spirit and moneybags behind the Liberal Party. Rowntree hired him as his confidential secretary.

On Rowntree's insistence the Party chose Lincoln as its candidate to stand for Parliament at Darlington, a teeming county borough on the Skerne near its junction with the Tees. To his own great amazement, Lincoln won and marched in triumph into the Mother of Parliaments. His two years as a back-bencher are best recorded by a cartoon in *Punch* that showed him in the proper morning coat, delivering one of his fiery speeches in the House of Commons. The caption under the cartoon read:

"Paks Vobiscum; or, The Lincoln Handicap—
" 'We weel not zend Budg-ett to ze Haus of Lorrdz to be zrown out only again!' (Mr. I.T.T. Lincoln—born at Paks in Hungary)."

At the end of his term, Lincoln was out of the House and flat broke. He then made a highly publicized trip to Hungary on what he described as a secret mission. Upon his return to London, he called on the First Lord of the Admiralty and revealed that he had brought back a mysterious formula capable of ensuring easy victory in any future war. He demanded a million pounds sterling for it, but was turned down.

"We never give any large amounts of money for secrets," the First Lord told him pointedly. "You see, Mr. Lincoln, we invariably know within a fortnight the secret of any invention or process in any navy in the world. So I must necessarily assume this to be the case with your secret formula as well."

Bidding him good-by, the First Lord then told Lincoln: "By the way, sir, I would appreciate it if you would return to my possession the Admiralty stationery you slipped into your pocket in the anteroom."

When World War I broke out, and Britain failed to win it overnight because presumably it had neglected to buy his secret formula, Lincoln volunteered his services in any capacity and was hired for the Hungarian section of postal censorship. Thus afforded an opportunity to gain some insight into the much-vaunted British Secret Service, he decided to become a spy for King and Country. But the stuffed shirts of that arrogant organization turned him down, too.

The series of humiliations he had to endure in Whitehall made him bitter and, in his spite, he turned against his adopted country. He developed a grandiose scheme to smash British seapower in a single naval action compared with which Trafalgar and Jutland would have been yacht races. In preparation for his fantastic coup he established contact with a German consul named Gneist who headed the Kaiser's espionage organization in Rotterdam. He also maintained a tenuous link with British Intelligence through a somewhat starry-eyed officer, Captain Philip W. Kenny of the "J" section of M.I.5, the espionage branch of the War Office.

Somehow he managed to persuade Captain Kenny that he

had access to the files of the German General Staff, and Consul Gneist that he was privy to the most closely guarded secrets of the British Admiralty. To keep both Kenny and Gneist happy, he sent them impressive intelligence reports in a special code. He thus once cabled Gneist from London care of a mail drop called Weber in Rotterdam:

"Stock market disorganized on account of Russian reverses stop Your holding following quotations colon 169/39, 239/15, 21/45, 129/10, 144/22, 119/39, 92/15, 239/36, 237/21 stop Signed Laming." The "quotations" were entries from his code book and translated into, "Raid will be made on island fortress of Helgoland in a week."

Using the same transparent self-made code, he cabled Captain Kenny from Rotterdam: "Prices too high stop Am willing to close as follows colon 92/02, 70/019, 140/07, 217/33, 124/026, 91/13, 93/5 stop Signed Bullock." It was supposed to mean, "Four divisions of new German troops leaving for France."

Thus firmly entrenched in both German and British confidences, Lincoln set the stage for the scheme he expected would hand victory to the Germans on a silver platter. His plan was to lure the British fleet to a certain spot in the North Sea where the Germans would ambush and annihilate it.

He told Captain Kenny he had to go to Rotterdam again to pick up some momentous intelligence and even procured a *laisser passer* from him so that he could travel unmolested by British counterespionage. Upon his return to London, he asked Kenny to put him in touch with the Admiralty because he had some world-shaking information for the Royal Navy. Kenny performed like a trained seal, but the Admiralty chose to ignore Lincoln. In a brazen act of supreme bravado, he complained to Winston Churchill, the First Lord himself. Apparently his complaint had the desired result. The next morning he received a wire from Captain Reginald Hall, the

Director of Naval Intelligence, inviting him to call at the Admiralty.

A man with a superb sense of humor as well as a sense of proportion, "Blinker" Hall saw through Lincoln and decided to teach him a lesson. Although he was fishing in the dark because he didn't know what Lincoln was up to, Hall frightened the daylights out of him by hinting ominously that he had a pretty good idea of his scheme. Old Blinker could have locked up Lincoln then and there but, as he himself put it later, he didn't want to dirty his hands with this miserable double agent. Instead of detaining him, he let him go, expecting that Lincoln would see the light and leave England on his own.

The strange meeting in Room 40 of the Admiralty's Old Building baffled Lincoln. He sensed that his game was up and he was flirting with disaster. He promptly moved out of his quarters on Torrington Square, then sneaked aboard a neutral ship and left for the United States just as Captain Hall hoped he would and good riddance. British seapower was saved!

In the United States, he claimed to be a major German espionage agent but succeeded merely in impressing a fellow countryman of his, the great publisher Joseph Pulitzer. He recognized a good story in Lincoln's adventures whether they were true or false. Pulitzer commissioned him to write a series of articles for the *World* exposing the diabolical machinations of the sordid British Secret Service.

Then Robert M. McBride, the publisher, invited Lincoln to enlarge his articles into a book, to be called "Revelations of an International Spy." He was working on his *magnum opus* when Captain Hall, realizing that he could have made a mistake when he permitted this shaver of the wind to go on the lam, reached out to get Lincoln back. He had him arrested in New York on a charge of forgery, an old trespass Scotland Yard had conveniently uncovered in Lincoln's untidy past.

He was thus forced to complete the book in the Raymond Street jail in Brooklyn (he eventually dedicated it to the warden), but by the time McBride published it, Lincoln was in a London jail. He was given three years and was then deported to Hungary. He was never again permitted to set foot on English soil, not even when he bizarrely requested permission to attend the execution of his only son, a chip off the old block. Junior was sentenced to death for complicity in murder. The refusal of those flint-hearted British to let him see his offspring hanged filled the cup of his hatred of perfidious Albion. He decided to go into the spy business with a vengeance and vowed to harm the British Empire wherever he could.

For a brief span, Lincoln fished in the muddy water of postwar Europe, ran errands for various Continental secret services, and eventually went to China, where he sold his services to anyone at all. He worked for the Japanese and played a dubious role in their conquest of Manchuria in 1931, while also working for the Chinese against the Japanese.

Far too conspicuous after a while for his chosen profession, he changed his religion again, was ordained a Buddhist priest and retired to a monastery in Tibet, where he hoped it would be rather difficult for the British to keep tabs on him. Then Hitler came to power and re-established the German secret service. Lincoln suddenly showed up in Berlin and tried to sell himself to the Nazis.

I met him during that sojourn accidentally. I was having coffee and *Schnecken,* a kind of Danish pastry with a Teutonic culinary twist, on the terrace of the Hessler on Potsdamer Platz when I suddenly saw a tall, gaunt, elderly man passing by. He couldn't help attracting attention because he was wearing the severe gray robe of a Buddhist monk with open-toe sandals, his smoothly shaved head and protruding beak making him even more conspicuous.

I jumped up and ran after him, and since this was Berlin, accosted him in German. He didn't respond. Flustered, I tried my French on him, then addressed him in English, but he kept mum. Suddenly it occurred to me that this tall old monk was a fellow Hungarian after all and I spoke to him in our native tongue. He stopped promptly and said:

"Young man, you've touched a soft spot. I shouldn't waste any of my precious time on insolent strangers like you, but I haven't had a chance for years to speak to anyone in the language of my forebears and, to tell the truth, I'm dying to speak a little Hungarian."

He looked at me sternly and asked: "Would you do me the honor of lunching with me?"

He took me to a little, second-story vegetarian restaurant on Potsdamer Street and insisted over a big plate of such raw delicacies as lettuce, celery and carrots that he was nothing but a Buddhist monk who was awfully homesick for Paks.

From Berlin he returned empty-handed to some godforsaken place in Asia and became the abbot of his order, which, the British claimed, consisted solely of himself and was just a blind. By then he was a tired old man who had more or less outlived his uselessness to all except maybe Siddhartha Gautama, the Great Buddha. The last time his name popped up in the newspapers was when they printed his obituary. Yet there are those who still insist that the fabulous Trebitsch Lincoln continues to haunt, like a vindictive ghost, the shadowy underworld of international intrigue.

It was Lincoln during our chance meeting in Berlin who expounded to me the basic philosophy of these shavers of the wind. We spoke about the precarious state of the world, and he blamed the so-called common man for his own misfortune in the hands of unscrupulous statesmen, for whom he had nothing but contempt.

"Beloved son," he said in the sanctimonious singsong of a

Buddhist priest, while speaking in Hungarian, "there is a Latin saying that hits the nail on the head. The saying is, *Mundus vult decipit ergo decipiatur.*"

"What does it mean, Your Eminence?" I asked, treating the old buzzard to a highfalutin' title.

"The world," he said with bathos, "wants to be deceived, consequently it is being deceived."

(When my eleven-year-old son, a red-blooded American, read this chapter, he remarked: "Well, it seems you Hungarians have found a way to improve on the supposed truism that one can fool only some of the people and that only some of the time.")

Double Agent

WHENEVER I AM IN INNSBRUCK, THE LOVELY TYROLEAN CITY famed for its fountains, rococo churches and Alpine cable cars, I dine at the Stiftskeller on Maria Theresien Street. It is a de luxe restaurant in the cellar of a massive gray Franciscan monastery. In the Stiftskeller the friars do all the work. They do the cooking, wait on the tables and wash the priceless old dishes with devout care. It is a delight to watch the portly waiters in their coarse monastic garb as they shuffle between the tables in their open-toe sandals, lugging huge trays with some of Europe's finest foods on them.

The place is a citadel of Austria's intricate *haute cuisine* but in Hungarian circles it is best known for an experience it once had with a distinguished guest from Budapest. He happened to be a friend of mine, a *bon vivant* of the old school, Józsi von Orkeny (as I shall call him), to whom the realities of our changing world held no meaning.

On the night of that particular incident Józsi arrived at

the Stiftskeller and was duly escorted to a reserved table, the best in the house. He ordered a glass of fragrant apricot brandy and sipped it pensively, like a chess master contemplating a move, while he chose his meal with his customary discrimination.

He began the historic dinner with Senegalese soup and had cold mountain stream trout *à la Floris* for his fish course. He continued with broiled guinea hen *forestière* on crisp toast, with puff balls of potatoes puréed with egg and large pine mushrooms sautéed in olive oil and garlic. He then had a pudding *à la Nesselrode,* brought to his table in an eerie little blaze made of the best Caribbean rum, served with candied fruits, perfumed strawberries and Malaga grapes.

He had Pabst-Traenen 1907 with the trout and Roussette de Seyssel 1911 with the guinea hen, cognac and a demitasse of imported Mocha after the meal, devoting well-nigh three full hours to his monumental culinary maneuver. When it was over at last and the time came to ask for the check, Józsi lighted a huge Havana Caballeros, beckoned to the genial friar who had waited on him, and said:

"Brother Aloysius, I would like to confess."

Moved by his guest's apparent piety, the friar led Józsi to a little chapel upstairs and eased him into a confessional.

"Brother," Józsi said as soon as he was settled in the stall, "I have to confess that I don't have any money to pay for the dinner."

This startling pronouncement was fraught with complications, both spiritual and temporal. Józsi's confession was, of course, a deep ecclesiastical secret the friar was not supposed to share with his brethren; but it also had certain secular ramifications.

"Blessed be ye poor," the hapless friar said, "but if you have no money, mein Herr, please kindly tell me why did you have to dine in a restaurant as expensive as the Stiftskeller?"

"I am a Hungarian nobleman, Brother Aloysius," Józsi said with reproach in his voice, "and for a Hungarian nobleman the best is not good enough."

Recalling Józsi's venture, I was surprised on a recent visit to Innsbruck to find him back at the celebrated cellar, engaged in the autopsy of a dazzling duckling *à la Metternich* in pungent kirsch sauce with pitted black cherries. Evidently that old incident of some twenty years before had left no hard feelings. The friars doted on him and devoted most of their time to serving him, letting the rest of us wait for our roast quails, goose Chateaubriand and other famed *specialités de la maison.*

Józsi spotted me at once and sent a jolly old flatfooted friar to my table with an invitation to join him. He received me with an exuberant show of affection, then turning to the friar, said:

"Brother Hyeronimus, this is an old school chum of mine I haven't seen for ages. This calls for a celebration. How about bringing up a bottle of Linzer Blut you have reserved for extra-special occasions?"

To tell the truth, I was just a bit apprehensive because I feared he had asked me over to pick up his tab at the end of the celebration. But I was to be pleasantly surprised. This time Józsi did not pay for our meals with a whispered confession upstairs. When the hefty check was sheepishly presented by the head friar, he peeled off the price from a big bundle of thousand-schilling notes, leaving one for the merry friars who had waited upon us.

I didn't know what to make of his sudden affluence. The last time I met Józsi, he was what Franklin Roosevelt once, in a vastly different context, called the forgotten man at the bottom of the economic pyramid. But his poverty was neither his vice nor his fault. It was rather an inconvenience caused by the caste system of Hungary's landed gentry, whose ancient family rules were not always supported by adequate funds.

My friend Józsi was the son of a vested landowner with arch-conservative principles. Old Orkeny stubbornly refused to concede that his venerable clan was living, not merely on borrowed time, but mostly on borrowed money. The Orkenys' ancestral domain of seven thousand hectares bordered on the Danube on one side, but otherwise it was surrounded entirely by mortgages.

Józsi's misfortune was not confined to the lamentable fact that he happened to be the offspring of an impoverished squire. It was aggravated by an added accident of birth. He was the fourth son, a genealogical position as unenviable in a Hungarian as in a Chinese Mandarin's family tree.

In Hungary, fourth sons of the landed gentry hardly had any standing in society or purpose in life. Succession and inheritance were strictly regulated by traditional estate laws. Under them, eldest sons inherited title and land; second sons went into such self-supporting vocations as the army, the clergy or government; and third sons became lawyers and doctors, or married American heiresses. Fifth and subsequent sons were so removed from this dynastic order that they had no choice but to go to work, mostly in commerce or high finance, pursuits frowned upon by their ancestors and elders.

The system thus left fourth sons in a category all by themselves. At one time I believe it was suggested that a kind of euthanasia be applied to the supernumerary issue of the lower nobility by drowning them at birth like the excess of a cat's litter. The idea was dropped when it was found to be illegal. Left to face the special hardships of their existence, the unfit had to engage in a struggle for survival as best they could.

Thus came into being a special social stratum, a group of titled playboys on pleasure bent, doing nothing useful in particular but doing it with exceptional taste and elegance. Nobody knew how they managed it, but these fourth sons lived extremely well, usually beyond the means of their friends.

A member of the caste in excellent standing, Józsi also succeeded in carving out a tranquil career for himself. He was what could be called an accompanist. He accompanied his well-heeled friends on safaris to Africa, on trips of chance to Deauville or Monte Carlo, even on round-the-world trips, because he was an entertaining companion who knew how to spend money far better than those who had it.

In 1937, I was told, he became tired of the uncertainties of his existence and planned to blow out his brains, when a sudden opportunity made such a macabre solution unnecessary. The opportunity came in the form of an invitation to a hunt on a big estate in Zalaber. Józsi went, of course; massacred 118 quails and 38 pheasants; then stayed to play picquet with his host for eight years. The game was interrupted by the sudden arrival of the Red Army on its westward march in 1945. All of a sudden, Józsi lost everything, the friends who supported him, the headwaiter at Gundel's who allowed him to dine on the cuff, even the two heroic loan sharks who had inscrutable faith in him.

Seeing his old world crumble and feeling the pinch of a cruel new world, Józsi decided to turn his back on Hungary. A little older but much wiser, he migrated to Austria, where I found him dining in style at the Stiftskeller and paying for his dinner.

I was familiar with Józsi's penurious past but not with his evidently prosperous present, so when I found him with a bundle, I could not resist the tactless question:

"What happened, Józsi? How come you're in the chips?"

"Ah," he said with a subtly mysterious smile, "times have changed, old man, and *malgré moi*, I had to change with them. The good old days of Aranjuez are over! Today I am . . . well . . . let's say an entrepreneur and to tell the truth, I'm doing rather well at it."

Suddenly I realized that this Józsi sitting across from me

in the Stiftskeller was different from the lovable windbag I used to know. He had changed even in appearance. He used to be a bony big man with a ferocious Magyar moustache, resembling a barbarian warrior. And yet, there had been a softness in him, and a gentle, disarming charm that made him difficult, if not impossible, to resist. All that had changed. The barbaric moustache was gone and so was the softness. Now there was conceit and arrogance in his bigness. The subtle mystery in his enigmatic smile also flickered in his eyes. This was a different József, I thought, a hard, predatory, tough guy.

The morning after the dinner, I was awakened by a knock on my door in the Kaiserhof. It was the ominous knock of a furtive caller and when I opened the door, I found a tall, slim young man standing outside, pushing a badge under my nose.

"Smith," he said gruffly. "CIC."

He was Frank Smith, one of the investigators from the U.S. Army's Counter Intelligence Corps in Innsbruck.

"Come in," I said, and when he was in, I asked: "What do you want?"

"We have reason to believe," said darkly, "that you had dinner with Baron Orkeny in the Stiftskeller last night."

"Well, yes," I said, "but what business is that of yours? For your information, he's an old classmate of mine."

"I know," Smith flaunted his omniscience. "That's why I'm here." He looked at me sharply and asked: "Are you involved in any of his deals?"

"I'm sure I am not," I said, "but tell me, Smith, what deals is my friend József involved in?"

"You mean to tell me you don't know?" He was sincerely astounded.

When I assured him that I had no idea, he sat down on my bed and spelled out in some detail what József meant when he had told me that he was an entrepreneur. According to Smith, the erstwhile playboy was the biggest local operator in the shabby underworld of the cold war. He ran an underground railway that brought people from behind the Iron Curtain. He headed a syndicate smuggling coffee and nylon hose into Hungary. He sold dubious South American passports to people who had none. He managed a lively black market in foreign currencies. He ran a local employment agency for call girls and placed pretty young refugee women in houses of assignation throughout the Middle East. He had a different organization for every one of these enterprises and was making money on all.

"Naturally, we don't like what he's doing," Smith said, "but there is nothing we can do about it. It's a matter for the local police. He has ample protection, however. He operates with total impunity." He paused briefly, then said: "We're interested in him for an entirely different reason."

"What's that?"

"Well," he said somewhat hesitantly, "we have reason to believe that he's also engaged in espionage."

"Józsi a spy!" I exclaimed. "How delightful!"

"It isn't that delightful," Smith said, "because you see, he isn't spying for us. As a matter of fact, we have reason to believe that he's working for the Russ . . . I mean, for a foreign power."

"No," I protested with some vehemence. "That's impossible. Józsi may be a scoundrel and all that. But I know he's a red-blooded Hungarian patriot at heart." Smith received my protestation with a sardonic smile.

"Didn't someone once say," he asked, "that patriotism is the last refuge of a scoundrel?"

"Samuel Johnson said that," I told him, "but the old doctor was an Englishman and didn't know Hungarians."

Smith just shrugged. "I really don't see why I'm telling you all this. After all, for all I know, you could be in cahoots with him. But in my job I have to operate on intuition. And my sixth sense tells me that I can trust you. Maybe you could help me get to the bottom of this."

He took a bundle of papers from his briefcase.

"Here," he said. "These are photostats of certain intercepts. They are letters the Baron wrote to an address in São Paulo, Brazil. We have reason to believe that the address is a mail drop."

He gave me one of the letters and asked: "What do you make of this?" When I was through reading it, I told him:

"My dear fellow, but this is ridiculous. Do you know what this letter is about?"

"I have the general idea," Smith said darkly.

"Why, it's nothing but the recipe of a delicious Hungarian dish. Here, for instance," I pointed out a line where Józsi wrote *nyul vadasmartasban*. "It means 'potted hare in venison sauce' or something to that effect. I am not an expert in these things but Józsi is. He used to be one of the most celebrated gourmets in old Hungary."

"That may be so," Smith said, "but this isn't old Hungary. Why the hell should he go to all this trouble sending these goddam 'recipes' to a mail drop in Brazil? This one, for instance," he said as he pulled another letter from the bundle. He tried to read something in Hungarian but when the words defied pronunciation, he spelled them out:

"P-a-l-a-c-s-i-n-t-a b-a-r-a-c-k-l-e-k-v-a-r-r-a-l. There just can't be any goddam words like these in any civilized language!"

"I'm afraid you're wrong, Smith," I said. "These are two perfectly respectable Hungarian words no cookbook would be without. They mean 'pancake filled with apricot jam.' "

"Or who knows, they may mean something else," Smith said. "We have reason to believe that this recipe nonsense is just a clever blind. The venison gravy, I mean, and all that pancake hogwash! We believe they are part of an ingenious code."

"You really mean it?" He was whetting my appetite.

"Yes. We sent the letters to our cryptoanalysts in Vienna and they agree with us this must be some code. But no matter how they tackled it, they couldn't break the damn thing. The problem is now with the National Security boys in Washington. They managed to break down this pal-a-chin thing into code symbols of the usual five letters each

PALAC
SINTA
BARAC
KLEKV
ARRAL

but they couldn't make any headway beyond that."

"Maybe it's really just a pancake recipe after all."

"That's what we would like to know," he said. "Maybe you could cuddle up to the Baron and find out what he's really up to with his unpronounceable recipes."

I agreed to break Józsi's code and decided to do it by asking him about it point-blank. He regarded the whole thing as a capital joke.

"It's just like that damn fool Smith, that imbecile," he said when he stopped laughing. "Those CIC characters see a spy behind every goddam tree. The guy in Brazil! You know him, too. He's our old friend Pista Blaha, you remember him, don't you? Fatso Blaha!"

"Of course I remember Fatso. He simply loved to eat."

"He's in the restaurant business in São Paulo. I'm helping him with special recipes from my private collection."

"Good for Pista," I said. "And if I know him right, he doesn't have to worry about any leftovers. Don't worry, Józsi. I'll clear you with the CIC."

"Why don't you tell Smith to stop spending the taxpayer's money on wild-goose chases. Instead of trying to break my code, he should give it to his wife to prepare for dinner."

He stopped abruptly, contemplating something that seemed to have popped into his head. Then he said, almost in a whisper: "But then, on the other hand, this thing gives me an idea."

That appeared to be the end of it. I told Smith what Józsi had told me and although he remained somewhat skeptical, he said he would file the case for the time being. A few weeks later I bumped into him at the Goldener Adler. He pulled me aside and told me in a low voice:

"Do you remember our little talk about those recipes?"

"Indeed I do. What happened? Did they upset your stomach?"

"Well, forget it."

"In other words Józsi is working for you."

"I wouldn't jump to any conclusions," he said. "Just forget the whole thing. It isn't important any more."

By then, the sudden brainstorm Józsi had when I confronted him with Smith's suspicion was paying him substantial dividends. He had added espionage to his other lucrative enterprises. "Why the hell didn't I think of it before," he would say. "It's so much simpler than any of the other things."

Józsi established himself in the business by purchasing a typewriter with a Hungarian keyboard and ordering from Budapest a couple of reams of bond paper with an unmistakably Hungarian watermark. He thus expected to give the impression that his intelligence reports originated inside Hungary, although in actual fact he made them up himself right there in Innsbruck. He culled information from the latest Hungarian newspapers, rewrote the items in special intelligence lingo until they sounded like spy reports, typed them out with the Magyar keyboard on the bond from Budapest, then peddled them to the various U.S. intelligence agencies in town. Smith became his first regular customer. The others followed soon afterward. A typical Józsi report looked like this:

"GG-107987-19-05, TOP SECRET, Subject: Airport, New, Building of; Area: Map 6X, Square 9, Pecs, Vicinity of. Source: MGM-305 (Highly reliable in the past). Courier: Barnacle. Route: IV/11 via II/37.

"Brief: According to informant MGM-305, a new airport is being built in the vicinity of Pecs (pop. 87,909) in SW Hung. 18.6 km. NE from Yugo border at Virovitica on Drava river.

"Loc. of airp. 46° 10 N, 18° 20 E. Runway 827 m, running SW-NE diagonal to control tower. Capable of accomod. propeller planes only. Ground firm, easily drained. Approaches unobstructed. Site reasonably unaffected by fog. Informant MGM-305 observed beacon lights, boundary lights, obstacle lights, wind indicators. Also spotted warning signals regarding storms, winds, in conspicuous places. During hours of darkness, informant MGM-305 observed illuminated wind indicators kept burning.

"Pecs is in vital coal-mining region. Informant WB-21A reports local Party secretary Gyorgy Boldizsar has illicit affair with secretary, Aranka Marosan. Will keep you posted developments."

The intelligence in this impressive report was based on a brief item in a Pecs newspaper that described the official inauguration of a new airport. The description was that of just any ordinary airport to which Józsi added a few educated guesses.

For a while Józsi operated full blast to the satisfaction of everybody concerned, including the Hungarian government, on whom he was supposed to be spying. But then, a few months later, when I happened to be in Innsbruck again,

Smith called me on the telephone. He asked me to come to his office at once.

"It's about the Baron," he said when I seated myself at his desk.

"Anything wrong?" I asked.

"I'm afraid plenty," Smith said. "We have reason to believe that he's a double agent working for the Hungarian secret police."

By then I was willing to believe anything about Józsi.

"Just what reasons do you have to believe it?" I asked in Smith's own vernacular.

"Well," he said, "lately he began giving us information of a more imminent value. About frontier crossings, for instance. And about unrest among the frontier guards, how some of them craved to defect to us. They were so glowing with optimism that they fooled even me. I sent a couple of my agents to a crossing in Square Eight that the Baron described as absolutely safe and what do you think happened?"

"What?"

"My guys almost fell into a goddam trap. They barely escaped with the skin of their goddam teeth. Then we tried to contact one of the Baron's would-be defectors in the Kormend zone of the frontier. What do you think happened?"

"What?"

"Far from being willing to defect, the goddam guard pulled a gun on my man and sounded the alarm."

This was bad business.

"Have you done anything to check out his information?" I asked.

"Not beforehand. After all," Smith said, "his previous reports all turned out to be reasonably reliable. But afterwards I put a tail on him and what we found merely deepened our suspicion. For one thing, we discovered he didn't have a single producing agent behind the goddam curtain. What do you think he did?"

"I have reason to believe he made up all his reports, typed them out on a Hungarian keyboard," I said, "and sold them to you."

Smith was amazed. Then he looked at me suspiciously.

"Are you sure you aren't in cahoots with him?"

"Pretty sure."

"Then don't you see? He's a plant! His job is to trap us!"

"Have you found an actual link between the Baron and the Hungarians?"

"No. None. But that's just it. He's a loner, don't you see? That makes him the more dangerous. He's so highly trusted they don't have to give him any instructions. No contacts. He operates on his own, as and when the occasion demands."

"Well, he's your baby," I said. "I really don't know what I can do to help you."

"This mess is awfully embarrassing to me personally," Smith moaned. "After all, I was the one who developed him. I'm loath to expose him because it would be, how shall I say, a reflection on me, getting caught with a double-A in my stable." He seemed to be desperately uncomfortable as he leaned over to me and said:

"To put it bluntly, I have reason to believe that I might even lose my job over this."

"Do you want me to talk to Orkeny?"

"Yes," he said eagerly. "You've been so helpful breaking the code. Perhaps you could find out directly from him whether he's really working for the Reds."

I called Józsi and invited him to dinner at the Stiftskeller that same night. I thought it was the appropriate locale for this denouement because that was where we came in. We had an exquisite meal, as usual, and another bottle of Linzer Blut that mellowed our mood. So it didn't sound quite so rude when I turned to him over cognac and Mocha, and said:

"Józsi, I'm afraid you're in trouble."

He looked at me with amusement rather than concern.

"Trouble? I'm used to trouble, my boy."

"But this is serious, Józsi. Smith thinks you're a double agent."

"A double agent?" he roared. "How the hell can I be a double agent when I am not even a bona fide agent in the first place?"

"Smith says they have reason to believe you palmed off misleading information on him to lure his men into a series of traps."

"For Pete's sake, old man! You ought to know me better! I would never do anything like that." He sounded almost honest. I was willing to give him the benefit of the doubt. But the evidence was still heavily weighted against him.

"Do you recall a report about the border guard near Kormend you said was simply itching to defect?"

"Yes," he said. "What about him?"

"Well," I said. "Smith sent one of his guys out to collect him but, as it turned out, the guard wasn't ready to defect, to say the least."

"Of course not," he exclaimed in righteous indignation. "I didn't mean my reports to be taken that seriously."

"Then why in God's name did you give them to Smith?"

"Because I could no longer stand their bloody defeatism. It made me sick to my stomach just looking at Smith's mournful long face. I was sorry for those poor idiots in CIC, G-2, CIA and the rest, everything going against them—the Sputniks, the Congo, Laos, Castro in Cuba! I decided to cheer them up with reports that sounded more optimistic. I gave Smith a report that said Khrushchev was suffering from lung cancer because he used to smoke too much. Now does that mean that Smith has to send a cancer specialist to Moscow? In another report I described how Janos Kadar was shot in a stormy cabinet meeting in Budapest. I spiced it up a bit and put in that he was shot in the behind."

"Was he?"

"Hell, no," he said impatiently. "But everybody else was giving them only bad news. I thought I'd give them a little good news for a change."

"Józsi, Józsi," I reprimanded him gently. "Poor Smith, he's in hot water now because of you."

"It serves him right," Józsi said. "Why couldn't he sit tight? And what kind of an intelligence agent is he, taking *my* reports so seriously. Tell your friend Smith he needn't worry. I'm not a double agent and I'm not working for the Reds."

He stopped abruptly, remained serenely silent for a moment, then said under his breath, as if talking to himself:

"But then, on the other hand, this thing gives me an idea."

The Scoop

DURING THE GOOD OLD DAYS WHEN BUDAPEST WAS STILL THE frivolous capital of a lighthearted country, the city had about one-sixth the population of New York, and maybe five times as many illiterates, but it supported some thirty daily newspapers, with as many axes to grind. Each of them represented a different political party or vested financial interest. Editorial policies reflected the sources of subsidies paid under the counter from mysterious unvouchered funds. Competition among the papers was brisk, both for the subsidies and for news. As a result, we reporters had to come up with scoops every day.

Crimes were solved for the next edition by intrepid reporters often before the arrival of the police on the scene, and cabinet ministers learned from the papers (including those they secretly subsidized) that their government had been overthrown.

Dryden's quip that some tell, some hear and some make news had real poignancy in Budapest, if only because much

145

of the news we told we had made up ourselves. On dull days when absolutely nothing newsworthy happened, enterprising editors like Arpad Vas would hire professional yeggmen to stage spectacular thefts, like stealing the crown jewels from their impregnable vault in the Royal Palace; or they would pressure the Foreign Ministry to declare war on some such country as Montenegro or Andorra, not an especially original scoop at that, after what Hearst pulled in Cuba in 1898.

Working on Arpad's well-subsidized paper, which featured an inexhaustible flow of scoops, I had my own quota of notable news stories, in line with my chief's motto, *Spargere voces in vulgum ambiguas,* which I owe to Vas's memory not to translate. Such a scoop of mine once created a nation-wide sensation. I revealed that certain tests given the girls at a fashionable finishing school on Szemere Street were in reality rabbit tests, necessitated by circumstances over which several of the young ladies had lost control. One of my scoops made history.

The chain reaction that led to this historic scoop began on a balmy spring morning that found me, as usual, at my regular table in the Café New York. Coffeehouses used to be landmarks in Budapest. The New York, in particular, was a national institution. Frequented mostly by practitioners of the seven arts, it was second only to the Royal Academy, although, of course, considerably more informal and somewhat easier to get into. If you happened to be a Bohemian, as we shiftless and usually impoverished intellectuals were called, your patronage was appreciated even if it did little, if anything, to enrich the management. Grand cafés like the New York, for example, and the Japan or the Abbazia, were our homes away from home, where we did our writing, transacted our business, had our flirtations, engaged in creative conversations, read the world press, and dreamed our fancy dreams. No limit was ever placed upon the length of our attendance, nor were we expected to consume anything more substantial than a

Kapuziner, a small glass of coffee with a little milk named after an order of friars, the Capuchins, whose coarse garb was black and white or rather *café au lait.*

A Bohemian could go to his regular café, sit down at his reserved table and tell the waiter in an imperious tone, "Bela, bring me a glass of water, some sugar and the London *Times,*" then produce a raspberry syrup, mix a delicious drink and settle down with the *Times* until it was time for another glass of water and maybe *Le Figaro* or the *Berliner Illustrirte.* On those rare occasions when we had a *prix fixe* dinner, we were allowed all kinds of substitutions, such as a couple of phone calls for the soup or a haircut instead of dessert.

The New York once introduced a special after-theatre dish called *lecho* that consisted of savagely spiced Debreczen sausages and was served with or without a rich goulash gravy. When the dish with its optional condiment first appeared on the menu, my friend Zoltan Baroti asked the waiter:

"How much is this lecho *with* the gravy?"

"A pengoe sixty-five, Mr. Baroti," the waiter replied.

"And how much is it *without* the gravy?"

"Also a pengoe sixty-five."

"What do you charge for the gravy?" Zoltan persisted, and the waiter said: "I guess the gravy is for free."

"All right, then," Zoltan said, "bring me the gravy."

This created a precedent, because afterwards we all indulged in lecho gravy whenever we happened to be hungry but short of cash.

Many a Hungarian writer or journalist, actor, painter or sculptor managed to survive because he had these well-lit, well-heated havens where he could sit out his lean years. They had an atmosphere of elegance and warmth, although in fact they were but shelters for destitute Bohemians, the Budapest version of Schrafft's and a Bowery flophouse rolled into one, with a built-in credit plan.

The cafés made their living from "civilians"—prosperous businessmen, doctors, lawyers and their ilk—who liked to be where the celebrities hung out. Those well-heeled philistines indulged in the various offerings of the house, paid promptly and tipped well, enjoying the normal comforts of a grand café in the proximity of famous people sipping their self-made raspberry drinks.

The New York was my regular hangout, but my presence in the place on this particular balmy spring morning was not entirely voluntary. As a matter of fact, I was there in what you could call enforced residence or maybe protective custody.

I had entered the New York the day before, planning to spend only a few careless hours at my usual table over a glass of *café melangé* with *schlag* and perhaps a crisp Emperor roll stuffed with thick slices of juicy Prague ham; read the *Melbourne Herald*, the *Neue Zurcher Zeitung* and the *Illustrated London News;* have a date with Luci Barna; discuss with my publisher the great Hungarian novel I hoped to write one day; and have a manicure downstairs. But when at 5 p.m. I asked Lajos, the debonair headwaiter, for the check, I found it amounted to forty-seven pengoes. It was a mysteriously exorbitant sum, especially for one who had only a couple of pengoes.

I was naturally scandalized.

"What do you mean," I asked Lajos, "forty-seven pengoes?"

"Two coffees, sixty fillers," he answered placidly, reading the items from a dog-eared index card, "a ham roll, one forty, arrears forty-five pengoes, total of forty-seven pengoes net."

"Don't be silly," I told Lajos. "Since when are you so hellbent on collecting arrears?"

"Since 1930, as far as you're concerned," he said with an acute sense of history.

"Look here, my dear Lajos," I said. "Actually I intended

to charge it, because I happen to have only a couple of pengoes on me. But since you seem to be in a mercenary mood, here, take your pound of flesh, but please loan me back a pengoe for the cab to my office."

"Your check is for forty-seven pengoes," he said darkly, "and I regret to inform you that you will not be permitted to leave the premises unless it is paid in full."

Eighteen hours after this sordid colloquy, I was still seated in the same place. At three o'clock that morning Lajos went home but left strict instructions with his relief to keep me in custody pending payment of my debt. In the meantime, I was permitted to add to it and thus my check grew to a little over fifty-five pengoes. I had a blue plate of cold cuts at 9:30 p.m.; a cup of chocolate and a cream puff, to which I treated Luci Barna, at midnight; a lecho *with* gravy at 4:17 a.m.; ham and eggs for breakfast at 8:45 a.m.; and seven cups of coffee in between. I also had my pants pressed, read eleven foreign dailies and the *Virginia Quarterly* from cover to cover, and made several phone calls, trying to contact someone who would rush to my aid. Needless to say, in vain. Each time I tried to sneak out, I was returned to my table by Geza the doorman, acting as a bouncer in reverse.

I did not have the slightest idea how I would ever solve this major financial crisis, for the sum Lajos demanded was enormous and my resources were at their lowest ebb. I could not figure out either why this trusting soul of a headwaiter had become suddenly adamant about collecting those arrears after so many years. In due course it developed, however, that Lajos had received secret intelligence that I was about to come miraculously into money within twenty-four hours.

Sure enough, shortly after eleven o'clock in the morning, Arpad Vas appeared at my table and fulfilled Lajos' expectations. I greeted Arpad effusively, like Dr. Livingstone must have welcomed Henry Morton Stanley in Ujiji, except that I felt I was really lost.

Arpad was all out of breath.

"So here you are!" he exclaimed. "I've been looking for you everywhere in town. Your landlady told me your bed wasn't slept in."

"No," I said with a smug smile, trying to soften the *denouement* of this encounter with my boss. "I spent the night in Luci Barna's apartment, but please keep it between us."

"You lucky dog," Arpad sighed, for Luci was the leading soubrette of the Royal Music Hall, in whose flat anybody would have liked to spend a night, Arpad more than anybody else. He then leaned over to me and said in a lowered voice:

"Listen, son. I've been tipped off that the army is holding secret maneuvers at Gyekenyes near the Yugoslav border. You know how explosive the international situation is. What with the assassination of the King and the issue in Geneva, these maneuvers have a special significance. The army prefers to keep mum but I want you to cover them."

He took a crisp new fifty-pengoe bill from his wallet and dangled it before my nose.

"Here," he said. "This will pay for your fare and a few incidentals on the trip."

"What class?" I asked.

"In a first class compartment I had reserved for you."

"You want me to cover the maneuvers of a whole army on just fifty lousy boodles?"

"Of course not," he said. "I've sent three hundred pengoes to the stationmaster at Gyekenyes, to be given you upon your arrival."

"I appreciate your confidence," I said, trying to keep the sarcasm of my feeling out of my voice. This was not the time to quibble about insults, however gratuitous.

"Find out what you can, but I doubt the army people will

let you use the regular facilities," he said. "These are top-secret exercises and the lid is definitely on. However, I've made an arrangement with a fellow named Imre Torok who is the chief conductor on the Budapest-Gyekenyes express. You just give him your uncensored copy in a sealed envelope and he'll bring it to me in the office on his return trip each day, as long as the maneuvers last. I can't be sure, of course, but I expect you'll be the only reporter on the spot. If you come through with this scoop, I'll give you a nice fat bonus."

"When am I supposed to leave?" I asked.

"The Gyekenyes express leaves Eastern Station at two thirty," he said solemnly. "I want you to be on it!"

"You can depend on me," I said, "but I have my check here to pay and unless I pay it in full, Lajos won't let me leave."

"Ridiculous," Arpad fumed. "What did you have?"

"Oh, a few cups of coffee, an Emperor roll with ham, and . . ."

"Never mind," he broke into my recital. "I'll take care of the check. Tell Lajos I'll pay it when I'm ready to leave."

I went over to Lajos, who followed developments avidly from a discreet distance, and gave him Arpad's message, but he demanded some more or less tangible assurance from Vas himself. I then arranged that Lajos would look in Arpad's direction and accept a nod from him as confirmation. A moment later this ingenious system of wireless communication was on. Lajos looked across to Arpad with eloquent eyes that asked: "Is it true that you'll take care of his check, the whole check, and nothing less than the whole check?" Vas responded with a prompt and vigorous nod of his head.

After my departure, I was later told, Arpad had ordered a light lunch and spent a couple of hours in the café writing his editorial for the next issue. When he was ready to leave, he asked Lajos for my check.

"What's this?" he exploded when confronted with those

fifty-five pengoes net. "Lajos! Are you trying to shake me down or something?"

"By no means, Mr. Vas," Lajos said with exquisite decorum.

"I was told he had only a few cups of coffee and a ham roll. What the hell are these fifty-odd chips for?"

"Arrears, Mr. Vas."

"I didn't agree to pay any arrears."

"Oh yes you did, Mr. Vas," Lajos maintained.

The crisis that followed somewhat overshadowed the trouble with Yugoslavia, but by then I was, presumably, on my way to Gyekenyes.

Unfortunately, this was one of those days. From the head-waiter's frying pan I fell headlong into my landlady's fire. After leaving Arpad at the New York, I rushed home to pack, but hardly did I have a few shirts and my razor kit in the valise when I felt the hot breath of my landlady scorching the back of my neck.

"What does this mean?" she asked me menacingly. "Don't tell me you're trying to sneak out on me!"

"By no means, Mrs. Leffler," I tried to reassure her. "I have to go to Gyekenyes, you see, to cover the maneuvers of the Royal Hungarian Army. It's really a stroke of luck. When I come back, Vas will give me a fat bonus from which I'll certainly be able to pay you whatever I owe."

"Do you realize you're five months in arrears with the rent?"

That word again. In Mrs. Leffler's steely, sharp voice it hit me like the cold blade of Dr. Guillotine.

"Of course I do," I said. "You won't let me forget it!"

"Well," she said in a stern voice that tolerated no contradiction, "you can't leave unless you pay!"

With that she left the room and turned the key in the door, from the outside. The situation struck me as far more serious than my similar plight in the New York. I was locked up like a character from Dickens, in a homemade debtors' gaol, with nothing to look forward to, not even a nod from Arpad in lieu of collateral.

When hardly an hour remained to make the train, I banged on the door and told Mrs. Leffler:

"All right, you win! I have fifty pengoes that Vas gave me for the first class fare. I reckon thirty pengoes will be enough if I go third class. Take the twenty, Mrs. Leffler, and let me out of here."

"Fifty pengoes!" she said in her icy voice.

There was nothing I could do. She refused to release me before I slipped the precious fifty under the locked door. I was free to do as I pleased, but down to two pengoes again—enough for a cab to the Eastern Station but woefully inadequate for the trip to Gyekenyes, where 300 pengoes waited for me.

All of a sudden the solution occurred to me . . . the chief conductor with whom Vas had made his arrangement!

I took the cab to the station and found Torok, the chief conductor, standing majestically on the platform, enveloped in the smelly steam of his train.

"Mr. Torok," I told him, "I'm the guy who's supposed to give you those letters for Mr. Vas, you know what I mean."

"Pleased to meet you," he said. He was a tall, broad-shouldered, brisk man in his late fifties, looking like a general in his neat uniform. "I've a compartment reserved for you."

"Unfortunately," I said, "I won't be able to go."

"What do you mean you won't be able to go?" He sounded beaten, his unexpected side income going up in the steam of his train.

"It doesn't matter, really, whether I go or not," I said, perhaps subconsciously outwitting the insulting precautions of my editor. "I can cover those blasted maneuvers without actually being present in Gyekenyes. Where do you live, Mr. Torok?"

"In Ujpest," he said. It was a nearby working-class suburb.

"Do you have a spare room you could put me up in for a few days, maybe a week?'

"It so happens that I have," he said. "I had to get rid of our regular boarder because he was getting too fresh with my wife. He paid thirty pengoes but you can have it for twenty-five."

"Fine," I said. "Now listen carefully. This is what we're going to do, you and I. You go to Gyekenyes, see the stationmaster, pick up the three hundred pengoes he's holding for me, deduct thirty pengoes for the room, then give me the rest when you get back to Budapest, tomorrow morning."

"But how about the letters you're supposed to send back with me?"

"Don't worry, Mr. Torok," I said. "There will be a letter for Mr. Vas."

He called his wife to tell her about their new boarder, then yelled out in his stentorian voice "All aboard," boarded the train and left with all aboard except me.

The arrangement proved to be much better than I expected. Mrs. Torok turned out to be a vivacious young matron, and quite pretty too, with a pleasant disposition to boarders. What with her husband being so much older and anyway spending but one night each week at home, she felt somewhat neglected. She received me with open arms and made me comfortable in every respect.

The morning after at seven thirty, Torok arrived back home on schedule, with my money from the stationmaster. I pumped him for whatever information about the maneuvers he had picked up while waiting for the turn-around of his train in Gyekenyes. It was enough for my first story. I typed it out, then sent it to Vas with the chief conductor, who delivered it on his way to the station to take the two thirty express back to Gyekenyes. When my first scoop appeared in Arpad's paper, the other papers also sent correspondents to Gyekenyes. After that I could use their dispatches, too, in addition to the items Torok was bringing me, so that I could season my stories with a few exclusives.

This went on for several days, the arrangement working perfectly for all concerned, except the army authorities, who were rather puzzled and annoyed when they found my uncensored dispatches splashed on the front page. They detached a whole division to make a frantic search for me all around Gyekenyes but, of course, they could not find me because I was under cover.

Everything went according to plan, until that Tuesday morning when seven thirty came and went without a sign of the chief conductor. When he didn't show up by ten o'clock, I persuaded Mrs. Torok to call Eastern Station and find out what was keeping her husband. There wasn't much they could tell her, but it seemed more was missing than just a chief conductor. She was told that the train her spouse had conducted so faithfully to and from Budapest for more than twenty years was also missing. The railroad was as mystified as we were by the sudden disappearance of a whole train, especially one that was hardly ever more than a couple of hours late on its regular five-hour run.

I had the morning papers but they didn't clear up the mystery. If anything, they deepened it. For one thing, they carried none of the daily specials from their men on the spot; for another, they printed angry editorials blasting the army, whose reactionary censorship, they claimed, was evidently responsible for this sudden dearth of news to which the public was entitled.

Later the afternoon papers came out with big black headlines about the "mystery of Gyekenyes," but had nothing with which even to hint at its cause.

I remained on pins and needles until two o'clock in the afternoon when the phone rang, someone from the railroad administration calling Mrs. Torok.

"Please don't get excited," a mournful male voice told her, "but I'm afraid I've bad news for you."

"What bad news?" she asked. "Is it about Imre?"

"There was an accident just outside Gyekenyes, Mrs. Torok. Your husband's train collided with a troop transport in what looks like the worst disaster in the whole history of the Royal Hungarian Railroads."

"A disaster!" she gasped and dropped the receiver, falling to the floor in a dead faint. Business before pleasure, I caught the phone.

"What happened?" I asked, and the voice went on officiously, apparently attributing to grief the sudden change of Mrs. Torok's voice from silvery soprano to beery baritone.

"We don't have all the details," the voice said, "but it seems that last night at seven thirty-seven a fully loaded troop transport of thirty-five boxcars carrying the entire Seventh Regiment was switched into the path of the express some five kilometers northwest of Gyekenyes. It was too late to avoid a crash! It's too horrible for words! General Szatmary died in the crash and I am sorry to say, Mrs. Torok, your husband is among the missing. We really don't know what happened to him. He may be alive and well, for all we know, because there are still hundreds in the two wrecks we are trying our best to extricate."

"How many dead?" I asked.

"We don't have the exact figures yet, but over two hundred bodies have already been identified. Now, Mrs. Torok, this is of course solely for your own information. You mustn't tell a word about it to anyone! The military authorities have ordered a total blackout of news. Nothing will be revealed until the Prime Minister himself goes on the air with a special announcement some time tomorrow. Chin up, Mrs. Torok!"

My hostess, for whom these words of sympathy were meant, was no longer prostrate on the floor. She was sitting in a chair, her chin way up.

"Darling," she said in an amorous whisper. "What a strange quirk of fate. Now that poor Imre is gone, bless his soul, you and I . . ."

I didn't wait for the end of the sentence.

A moment later I was flying low in a cab, taking the biggest story of the year personally to Budapest. I dictated it straight into a linotype machine, then sat back, warming myself on the nice fat bonus Vas had handed me in an improvised ceremony, the whole office assembled in the city room to witness my moment of triumph.

The blackout was blacker than ever when our paper appeared in the streets with a succession of extras, the shrill, excited voices of the newsboys penetrating to us upstairs.

". . . extra, extra . . . read all about it . . . worst railroad accident in history . . . hundreds dead . . . crack regiment wiped out . . . famous general among the victims . . ."

Arpad was making a speech.

"My boy," he said, looking at me with moist paternal eyes, "your deed is certain to go down in the history of journalism. You not only clinched the story of the year in an exemplary fashion but also delivered it, letting neither snow, nor rain, nor heat, nor the gloom of night prevent you from the completion of your appointed round. My boy," he raised his voice, "you make me proud to be a newspaperman!"

"It's you, sir, who deserves the praise," I responded modestly. "After all, it was you, Mr. Vas, who found out about the secret maneuvers and sent me, a little reporter, to cover it."

"True, true, my boy," Arpad said, catching the ball. "I do have an awfully good nose for news."

Just then, he was called away to answer a call. When he returned to our impromptu celebration, he seemed a bit puzzled, as he whispered to me:

"It was Torok, you know the fellow, the chief conductor we had the arrangement with. He was flown to Budapest and just reached his house in Ujpest. He said he couldn't find you there so he won't have anything for me this time. What did he mean?"

"Poor chap," I said, "he must be in shock."

"Yeah," Arpad said.

"Delirious," I said.

That seemed to settle it, but just in case, I left the party abruptly to cash my nice fat bonus check before that confounded conductor came out of shock.

Mustering

SOME PEOPLE LIVE DANGEROUSLY BUT JUST GRIN AND BEAR it, like the Japanese, for example, who never know when an earthquake or a typhoon may devastate them. In my time, Hungarians also lived in the shadow of instant death. They could never know when they would be quartered by a dashing officer of the Hussars or, for that matter, even of the infantry. I really mean it. Literally quadrisected.

Under the medieval code of honor that survived intact into the twentieth century, it was not merely the privilege but the bounden duty of members of the Hungarian officers' corps to avenge any personal insult on the spot by drawing their fearsome swords and cutting down the offender. It was left to the discretion of the offended officers to judge the situations and act upon them.

If no massacres resulted from this feudal system, it was not on account of any lack of determination on the part of our gallant officers to strike when aroused. One deterrent was that civilians exercised extreme caution when dealing with officers. Another was a certain discrepancy between the old officers' code and the criminal law.

The system fell more or less into disuse when a young cavalry captain named Huba Bator was given the Meritorious Service Medal by the army and thirty-five years by the Criminal Court for making slices of London broil out of a loan shark who had dunned him. Captain Bator considered it an insult to be reminded of his debts. He availed himself of this prerogative not merely to avenge a reflection on his honor but, more specifically, to get rid of one of his creditors.

The right to quarter civilians was just one of those things that made the army vastly unpopular with the population. Universal conscription was another. People tried their best to evade military service. They migrated to America by the thousands, for even hard labor in the bituminous coal mines of darkest Kentucky was regarded as preferable to service in the Royal Hungarian Army. Those who couldn't afford even steerage to the States resorted to all sorts of tricks and subterfuges to bamboozle the army doctors. The situation became so bad that the medics took in anybody who remained standing during the physicals. Even terminal cases thus got into the army, labeled as malingerers. Examinations were tightened only when the mass death of malingerers led to embarrassing questions in Parliament.

A sigh of relief went up in the country when, after Hungary's defeat in World War I, the peace treaty of Trianon abolished conscription by restricting the army to a very small professional force of bona fide volunteers. It seemed that the peril of military service was averted, and people breathed easier—until it became a fad in Europe to violate peace treaties.

Thus, I wasn't trying to escape military service when I decided to move to Berlin for good. To all appearances, conscription was not merely frowned upon but actually outlawed in

Hungary. I was, therefore, rather surprised when told by a nice Hungarian consul in Berlin that he could not extend my passport unless I presented myself in Budapest to be mustered into the army.

"Just what do you mean?" I protested. "As far as I know, there is no more conscription in Hungary and I certainly don't intend to volunteer."

"That may be so," the consul said with an impish smile. "But you can't have your passport extended unless you produce documentary proof that you have served your stretch in the army."

"What army?"

"I guess the Royal Hungarian Army. What else?"

"But it doesn't exist."

"That's a matter of opinion," he said curtly. "In my opinion you don't exist either. So how can I extend a passport for someone who doesn't exist?"

Clearly I had no choice. I had to go to Budapest and have myself mustered, as this sneaky way of creating volunteers for Hungary's non-existent army was officially called.

I figured I would take care of the matter over a weekend, going home on a Friday, presenting myself for mustering on a Saturday and returning to Berlin immediately afterwards. I had no doubt that I would have myself found unfit for any kind of military service. My first contretemps came when I arrived in Budapest. I was told that musterings were held only once a month and I had just missed the last by a couple of days.

I still didn't despair. I was working for the Berlin bureau of a big American news agency and assumed that the Hungarian authorities would be embarrassed if the existence of their non-existent army were so conclusively revealed to an American press association reporter.

I went to the Foreign Ministry in Buda where I had a friend,

Dr. Ferenc Mengele by name, the chief of the Press Department.

"Look, Feri," I told him. "You have to do something for me. I'm being mustered into the army."

He seemed startled. "What army?" he asked.

"Well," I said a bit testily, "it doesn't look to me like the Salvation Army."

"I really don't know what you're talking about," he said in his most officious tone. "As you well know, Section VII, Article 3, of the Treaty of Trianon forbids us to maintain a conscript army. And as you ought to realize as a patriotic Hungarian citizen," he raised his voice and looked firmly into my eyes as he invoked my patriotism, "as a good Hungarian you ought to know that the Royal Hungarian Government is scrupulous in its observance of the pertinent provisions of the said peace treaty, no matter how degrading and humiliating they are for a country as chivalrous as our beloved fatherland. So . . ."

"So what?" I asked eagerly.

"So there isn't anything I can do for you," he said, "except to sympathize, my dear chap. It seems to me you must be suffering from some sort of hallucination or delusion, and if you persist in talking about 'mustering' and 'army' you might wind up in a psychiatric ward."

"What do you suggest?" I played along.

"I suggest that you see a psychiatrist," he said, "preferably Dr. Paul Hansburg, and tell him Mengele sent you."

The drift of Mengele's suggestion quickly penetrated my not too naïve nature, and I hastened to follow the indicated course.

Dr. Hansburg made me lie down on a couch and fired the familiar questions at me. "Do you hate your mother?" he asked for a starter.

"What has that got to do with this delusion of mine?"

"A lot," he said. "Momism is a rather comprehensive analytical term. There are a number of mother symbols and, according to Professor Winterstein, the distinguished Viennese psychiatrist, the army is definitely one of them. At any rate, we're looking for the syndrome, so to speak. We have to put our diagnosis together bit by bit, like a mosaic, so to speak. Other important symptoms are nail-chewing and things like that. Incidentally, have you been wetting your bed lately?"

"I don't think so, but now that you mention it, I think I've been doing quite some nail-chewing ever since this delusion hit me."

"Aha," he exclaimed triumphantly. "Any unusual dreams?"

"I'm glad you asked me that. I did have a strange dream the other night. I dreamt I was a little fish swimming upstream in the Danube. Then a fellow who looked like the consul in Berlin appeared with a big tackle and caught me. Sometimes on rainy days I still feel the bite of his hook in my palate."

"Aha," Dr. Hansburg said. "I think I have your syndrome. You *are* suffering from a delusion, not quite dementia praecox, of course, but a distinctly paranoid phenomenon caused by morbid anxiety and a dash of persecution complex. I suggest that you see me three times a week for the next five years and we'll see what we can do for you. In the meantime," he added, "I will talk to my friend the Surgeon General to refrain from aggravating your condition by mustering you into anything even remotely resembling an army."

At last I had an alternative. I had the choice of serving either five costly years on Dr. Hansburg's couch or two years in the army for free. After the session, the army appeared rather attractive to me, which, of course, could have been but another symptom of acute hallucination.

My choice was made easier when, upon returning home, I found an official-looking letter waiting for me. It was from an agency called the Royal Hungarian Tourist Association, instructing me in no uncertain terms to appear in the Count

Hadik Barracks in the morning of May 27, with my gear, to participate in a patriotic excursion that could last for two years.

It was ten in the morning on the appointed date when I walked through the heavy oak gate of the Hadik Barracks, looking for the travel bureau in charge of patriotic excursions. A sentry stopped me inside the gate.

"Mustering?" he asked gruffly.

"No," I said. "Excursion."

"Room two-oh-seven," he said.

I had to go along a corridor that opened at my left on the huge courtyard of the barracks. Down in the yard squads of fellow travelers, dressed in ill-fitting, dirty fatigues, marched up and down, apparently practicing for the excursion. They were supervised by tough-looking sightseeing guides wearing sergeants' uniforms. The tourists looked awfully grim. I couldn't see a smile on a single face. Yet they sang lustily and loudly, a song that sounded like:

> *Hi, hoy*
> *Life in our army is sheer joy!*
> *Tip, top*
> *Hungarian recruits are the cream of the crop!*

I found Room 207 at the end of the corridor, knocked and waited until a stentorian voice bid me enter. I found myself in a brightly illuminated room that resembled the operating theatre of a hospital. There were two army officers and a sergeant in the room, and five boys about my age, standing at attention in their birthday suits.

I showed the sergeant my invitation and he passed it on to one of the officers, a lieutenant colonel of the Medical Corps, who turned on me:

"You were supposed to be here at seven o'clock," he

boomed, and I boomed right back: "What difference does it make? As a matter of fact I only came as a matter of courtesy to tell you personally that I'm not interested in this excursion of yours."

The colonel stared at me with incredulous eyes.

"What did you say?" he asked. "You aren't in-ter-es-ted?"

"Yes. I am not. You see," I told him firmly, "I have no time for excursions. I'm expected back at my job in Berlin, so please, sir, let's get this over with as quickly as possible."

It took some time for the colonel to find his voice, but when he found it at last, it was more booming than ever.

"Sergeant!" he roared.

"Yessir, Mr. Lieutenant Colonel," the sarge shouted back, jumping to attention.

"This man here," the colonel yelled at the top of his voice. "He's in a hurry. So let's fix him up real nice so that he can go back to Berlin as quickly as possible."

"Yessir, Mr. Lieutenant Colonel," the sergeant roared.

I thought I saw a sadistic smile sneak on the colonel's face, as he suddenly lowered his voice and said with exaggerated courtesy: "I recommend this young man to your special attention, Sergeant Fenyo. Make him as comfortable as possible."

"Yessir, Mr. Lieutenant Colonel," the sarge yelled, clicked his heels, then grabbed me by the arm and dragged me out of that room into another. A big, dimly illuminated hall, it was crowded with men of my age, standing awkwardly in their bare pelts, like newcomers to a nudist convention, exuding apprehension and body odor.

"Take your things off and wait here," the sergeant yelled and left.

I looked around for some solace and saw a sentry standing at the door, with a bayonet on his rifle. I went up to him and asked:

"Is there a place here one can make a phone call?"

"Why?" the sentry asked.

"Because I have to call His Excellency Dr. Ferenc Mengele in the Royal Ministry of Foreign Affairs."

It must have impressed him because he said:

"There's a phone in the canteen. But make it quick!"

I found the canteen and called Mengele.

"Listen," I told him, "I'm here in the Hadik Barracks at what seems to me the terminal stage of my schizophrenia. What's more, I'm on the verge of being mustered into the army on a two-year excursion."

Before Mengele could invoke the pertinent stipulations of the Treaty of Trianon, appeal to my patriotism and reiterate that I was sick, sick, sick, the sergeant burst into the canteen, accompanied by two husky military policemen.

"There he is," the sergeant roared, "the lousy deserter!"

"How can I be a deserter," I ventured to say, "when I'm not even in the army yet and not in an army, at that, which doesn't even exist?"

"Shut up!" the sergeant shouted. "Okay, men," he told the two army cops, "arrest the guy!"

"Wait a moment," I suddenly heard a voice say from a dark corner of the canteen. "Let me handle this, Sergeant Fenyo."

The voice belonged to a heavy-set, broad-beamed old man. He ponderously approached this outlandish scene and took charge in a manner that clearly indicated he was used to such emergencies. He turned out to be old Takacs, the concessionaire of the canteen, but apparently his authority extended far beyond his drab mess. His intervention stopped the sarge in his tracks.

"Okay, men," he screamed at the cops, "scram!" Then he turned to the old man and said with a servitude I didn't think he was capable of: "I guess it'll be all right to leave him with you, Mr. Takacs, but please don't forget to cut me in. I'll be waiting outside."

"So you don't want to go into the army," the old man said when we were alone.

"It isn't that I don't want to," I said cautiously, "but first of all, I don't like to be shanghaied like this, and second of all . . ."

"Never mind," the old man said. "How much sugar have you on you?"

"How much what?"

"Hard cash."

"Why?"

"I gotta know if I can do anything for you."

I looked into my wallet and pulled out three big bills.

"I have three hundred pengoes on me," I said.

"It ain't enough," Takacs grunted.

"I can give you a check."

"No checks."

"What do you suggest?"

"I dunno," he said, but I could see he was figuring something.

"How much do I need?"

"Well," he said slowly, "this is usually a five-hundred-pengoe proposition, but lemme see what I can do for you. Come inside."

He took me into a little back room and made me sit down on a chair.

"Open your shirt," he said. From a drawer he took something that looked like a piece of adhesive tape, cut a tiny disk out of it, then returned to me to contemplate my bare chest.

"Why do you have to have so much hair, goddamit," he said reproachfully, examining my chest thoroughly for a spot where he could paste up the little disk. He finally put it under the left nipple where the pink of the tape faded in with the skin. He stepped back, tilted his head, squinted and looked at the little patch like a connoisseur.

"It'll do," he finally said. "Okay, now, you just go back in and wait for your turn."

"What'll happen?" I asked.

"What do you expect for three hundred beans?" he said. "You could've been found unfit for good if you had the five hundred. As it is, you'll be deferred for a coupla years."

When my turn came, the sarge took me to the lieutenant colonel and said:

"He says something's wrong with his chest, sir."

The colonel looked at my chest, bare as the rest of me, except for that tiny pink disk under the left nipple.

"Acute case of herpes zoster," he dictated to the clerk. "Deferred for two years." He then turned to me and said: "You have to come back in a couple of years because your condition will clear up by then. Dismissed."

"Thank you, Mr. Lieutenant Colonel," I said, "but pardon me, sir."

"Yes?" he asked impatiently.

"Do I have to come back in person or . . ."

"Or what?"

"Or could I buy another one of these little pink disks right now and just mail it to you to show that I still have, whatever it is?"

"An acute case of herpes zoster," he said, then caught himself and yelled: "Get the hell out of here."

I left with springy steps and a light heart, humming as I went:

> *Hi, hoy*
> *Life in our army is sheer joy!*
> *Tip, top*
> *Hungarian recruits are the cream of the crop!*

The Duel

I WAS SITTING IN THE OSTENDE, AN OBSTREPEROUS CAFÉ FEA-
turing an oversized gypsy orchestra made up of swarthy child
prodigies, when disaster suddenly struck to the tune of the
Zigeunerweisen.

My only enemy in town suddenly came into the restaurant,
spotted me at once, and made straight for the table where I
was sitting and sipping a glass of *Egri Bikaver,* a red wine
named, in effect, the bull's blood.

He came to a stop, towering over me like an angry angel of
retribution, then demanded without further ado:

"Is it true that you called me a glorified pimp?"

"Well, yes," I replied foolishly, "but I put the accent on
glorified."

Before I could put up a more tangible defense, he slapped
me in the face and said, with the prescribed formality: "I trust
you are a gentleman and know what this involves. I expect
your seconds not later than five o'clock tomorrow afternoon."

Dueling used to be the favorite pastime of the Hungarian male in my stratum. Every self-respecting Hungarian male above the laboring classes had to have at least one duel to be socially acceptable. Those who knew what was good for them provoked trivial incidents with others they judged inferior in skill and fought perfunctory duels to get it over with.

Dueling was a violation of the law, but it was downright unpatriotic to take the law seriously. These affairs of honor were thus never shrouded in any mystery, for the legal sequelae of a duel were as much a badge of honor and chivalry as the duel itself.

Duelers were rewarded with a quaintly archaic sentence meted out in a special court by gentle magistrates. It was a week's sojourn in an ancient fortress at Vacz, high above the Danube, an idyllic resort of sorts where these "criminals" were the honored guests of the commandant.

This anachronistic chivalry had its strict rules. They were laid in a formal Code of Honor that resembled the rules of the Marquis of Queensbury. Under the rules, minor infractions, such as having one's toes stepped on or being called an oaf, required merely formal apologies. Certain second-degree insults called for swords, to be sure, but of the lighter variety, to be used in a genial encounter up to the drawing of the first blood.

My case was different. A slap in the face was regarded as the worst kind of insult. Not only was a duel mandatory, but honor called for heavy cavalry sabres to be wielded to the point of total exhaustion.

I must admit that the pageantry of the whole thing was not altogether unattractive, particularly in view of the fact that duels were so well managed that in the modern history of dueling in Hungary there had been only one fatality. The challenger in that encounter was stricken by a heart attack brought on by the excitement of the occasion. Nevertheless, I would have had more qualms about becoming number two on the fatality list if the prehistory of this affair had not had romantic overtones that blinded me to the possible consequences.

I was deeply attached to a very blonde young lady of excellent family and used to entertain her in a furnished room rented for the purpose when she was supposed to be attending piano lessons. While her skill at the keyboard made no appreciable progress under the circumstances, my feelings for her did, and I was even toying with the idea of marrying her—well, not necessarily marrying her, but getting engaged to her, maybe.

One day, out of the blue, she advised me she had decided to pursue her piano lessons in earnest. I was saddened by this sudden turn because she had no other time she could spare for me, but there seemed to be nothing I could do to alienate her new-found musical addiction.

A few weeks later I happened to bump into her piano teacher.

"I understand Mimi is developing into quite a virtuoso," I told her.

"Mimi?" she said. "I haven't seen her in months."

I made discreet inquiries and discovered that it was not the piano I had lost Mimi to, but a police captain. He was giving her the lessons she used to take from me. It was in first shock that I called the captain a "glorified pimp," although I knew, of course, that he was nothing of the sort. He steadfastly refused to take any money from Mimi beyond the few pengoes he needed to pay for the rental of the room where they met clandestinely three times a week. That was one time more than I had entertained her. The added tryst was made possible when Mimi told her parents she so enjoyed her lessons that she had decided to increase them from two to three a week, thus showing a zeal that pleased her father, but made her mother, who also used to take piano lessons in her youth, a wee bit suspicious.

So now I was looking forward to my dawn of destiny with mixed feelings. After my initial shock and subsequent disillusion I was no longer fond of Mimi and thought it rather foolish to spill my blood over her. In fact, I did not cherish the idea of spilling my blood on any grounds, even under general anesthesia. In addition, from early childhood on, I was myopic and had to wear heavy glasses. I couldn't see how I could give a good account of myself on the field of honor with my glasses off and blind as a bat.

But I had no choice. I had to go through with this thing even if it killed me—which was exactly what made me so apprehensive. I chose my seconds with extreme care, for much depended upon them. In a real sense, they held power over life and death. A shrewd second could lighten the burden of a duel by insisting on easier terms without violating the Code of Honor, while sanguine seconds, hell-bent on bloody murder in the guise of this idiot chivalry, could make things pretty bad.

Budapest had two distinguished gentlemen highly favored as seconds, known for their ability to lighten the burden. One of them was an attorney with hardly any practice, for he spent his time in sports-car racing as a semipro driver for Bugatti when he was not seconding at duels. The other was an obstetrician who had delivered his last baby some twenty-odd years before and now concentrated on preserving lives in this more exciting manner.

My seconds met my opponent's seconds in a private room of the Ritz Hotel the noon after my mishap and discussed the case for barely five minutes. Then my opponent and I were called in to hear the terms of the duel.

"In view of the fact," the spokesman of the seconds proclaimed, "that the insult in this case was of a physical nature, we are obliged under Article 27, Section 2, Paragraph 3 of the Code of Honor to arrange for a duel. It will take place at 4:30 a.m. on May 17th, in Studio Two of the Santelli Fencing School, with heavy cavalry sabres and without any protecting bandages, to total exhaustion."

I heard these stern words as though listening to my death sentence. I don't know what made me do it under those solemn circumstances but I asked: "Could not the terms be changed slightly?"

"What do you mean?" the four seconds turned on me in horror.

"Well, I thought maybe we could do it *with* heavy protecting bandages and *without* cavalry sabres."

One of my own seconds, the obstetrician, rose to reprimand me.

"This is not the occasion, sir," he said, "for jokes of this flippant character. I would like to impress upon you the seriousness of the matter and ask you to conduct yourself accordingly, or else," he went on, raising his voice, "we will be compelled under Article 98, Section 5, Paragraph 11 of the Code of Honor to disqualify you."

I got only a single break. In view of the fact that I had never before held a sabre in my hand and was a total stranger to the gentlemanly art of fencing, I was allowed four weeks to practice with a master of my own choosing. I chose Georgio Santelli, son of the owner of the studio where my duel was to take place, a friend and champion sabre-fencer, hoping against hope that he would be able to instill in me the skill and courage needed for this cruel ordeal.

Never did time fly faster than those four weeks. Before I knew it I was on the eve of my dawn of destiny. I was haunted by premonitions of disaster and death. I was convinced that my opponent would make mincemeat out of me, in the literal sense of the phrase, despite the devoted efforts of Georgio.

I was at my wit's end and even toyed with the idea of leaving Budapest altogether under the cover of darkness. But so power-ful was the spell of honor in Budapest that I came to dread escape from the duel even more than I dreaded the duel itself.

In my agonized state, then, I suddenly hit upon what seemed to me a brilliant idea. Dueling was illegal, wasn't it? Well, I would denounce myself to the police and they would have to stop the bloody thing under the law. I could not very well go to the police myself, so I chose my mother to do the de-nouncing for me. Under the Code of Honor, Article 19, Sec-tion 1, Paragraph 47, one was forbidden to reveal the im-pending event to anyone unless compelled to do so. I went to my mother's apartment and told her, obliquely but omi-nously, "I came to bid you farewell," in a solemn and mournful voice.

"Where are you going?" she asked, thinking probably that this being a Friday afternoon, I planned to go away for the weekend.

"Unfortunately, I am bound by honor not to tell you."

"Don't be silly," she said laughingly, "you used to tell me worse things than that."

"There can be no worse thing than this," I said darkly.

She flushed with excitement. "Are you by any chance going to have . . ." she asked, and I said with all the solemnity at my command: "Yes, mother."

She broke into a joyous smile that framed her whole face like a wreath, then stepped up to me, embraced me and said:

"My boy, I am proud of you! You know, I was getting a little bit embarrassed when all the sons of my best friends had their duels and you somehow never got around to one. Only the other day, Mrs. Kohner bragged to me about the duel of her son. I could have killed her. But now, I need not be em-barrassed any longer. Who is the lucky opponent?"

"Mother," I said frantically, "you don't seem to understand.

This is a deadly serious matter, *deadly*, you hear me! My opponent is a captain in the police department and he is certain to cut me to ribbons."

Unfortunately, the blood of old Hungarian chivalry flowed like wine in my mother's veins and I had a hard time, indeed, persuading her to denounce me. In the end, and with a broken heart, she went to the police department on the only such mission in the recorded history of Hungary. She was assured that a police officer would be sent to the Santelli studio in time to see what was cooking.

While previously I could not think straight, now I felt perfectly at ease. It was with a light mind and jaunty steps that I approached the Santelli establishment on Elizabeth Ring. It was four o'clock in the morning and the city was shrouded in vague predawn darkness. There in the darkness I saw the most welcome sight I ever hoped to see—a police car parked in front of the building.

Upstairs in the waiting room I found an even more welcome spectacle—a young police lieutenant yawning over a girlie magazine. When I entered he got up and asked me: "Sir, are you one of the gentlemen who'll have a duel here later?"

"Yes, indeed," I said with thinly concealed exuberance.

"Well," he said, "good luck to you, sir. We understand these affairs of honor. I'll get the facts and names after the duel."

I had little time left to sink back into despair because the others started drifting in—my seconds, my opponent accompanied by his seconds, then the two surgeons, and finally the sword-master in charge of the weapons. We all went into the studio, I, with rather unsteady steps, like a man walking his last mile. I was stripped to the waist by a dresser while the sword-master prepared the weapons. The two doctors were sorting their instruments on tables provided for this purpose. It was a ghastly sight.

Our seconds went into a last huddle in a far corner of the studio, then joined us to make the last-minute announcements. It was my obstetrician friend who acted as their spokesman.

"I have just had the honor of being chosen the Leading Second," said he, "by the drawing of lots as stipulated under Article 67, Section 5, Paragraph 13 of the Code of Honor. There will be only one change in the arrangements as previously announced. In view of the relatively minor nature of the original insult and the formal character of the retribution, it was unanimously resolved, in accordance with the pertinent provisions of the Code of Honor under Article 16, Section 2, Paragraph 1B, to change the duration of the duel from *total exhaustion* to *first blood*."

I was too far gone to appreciate this slight amelioration of the terms and had no time to contemplate its greater meaning. We took up our positions at our respective chalk marks, and with our swords held ceremoniously straight, pointing to the ceiling, we listened to the final pronouncements. The Leading Second was doing the talking:

"The gentlemen understand the terms of the duel and, having studied the pertinent provisions of the Code of Honor, undertake upon their words to abide by them. I am obliged under Article 101, Section 2, Paragraph 2 of the said Code of Honor to ask the gentlemen to reconcile." Then he continued without a pause (although I was rather eager to respond to his invitation) "The gentlemen *refuse* to reconcile."

Holding his sword like a maestro's baton, the Leading Second swept us through the rest of the performance.

"*En garde!*" the good doctor shouted at the top of his booming voice. And a second later: "Go!"

The nightmare lasted only the fraction of a moment. I had hardly time to swing my sword clumsily, when I heard the bellowing baritone of the Leading Second again, yelling: "Halt! Doctor! I think I see blood!"

I was ready to faint from the presumed loss of it when I suddenly noticed that my own doctor remained standing at his table while my opponent's surgeon was rushing to his side. The police captain, somewhat paler than usual, was led gently to a leather sofa at the wall and made to lie on his belly, while the doctor treated a four-inch flesh wound in the upper part of his left shoulder blade.

I could hardly believe my eyes. And I attributed it to my semicomatose condition that I could not remember my brilliant coup. But who was I to argue with chivalry. I was a hero! This was the triumph of David over Goliath! A short-sighted sad sack who never had a sabre in his hand—much less a heavy cavalry sabre—until four weeks before had drawn first blood in a duel with an opponent who virtually lived by the sword.

I rushed to the phone to call my mother.

It was the happiest day in her life, far happier, indeed, than the day when I graduated from the Peter Pazmany University *summa cum laude*.

Shortly afterwards I left Hungary for good, maybe because I decided to leave such good things alone and not to challenge fate with the prospect of another duel. I came to live in the United States, where many years later I happened to bump into the obstetrician who had been my Leading Second, a refugee survivor of a concentration camp.

We celebrated our reunion at the Hotel Berkley's bar, rehashing the memories of that supreme adventure at dawn.

I could not suppress a bit of bravado. "You know," I told him, "for a guy like me who had never indulged in sports and who had never handled a sabre before, it was pretty good for me to cut up that captain."

"The hell you did," the obstetrician said quietly.

"What do you mean?" I asked.

"I shouldn't tell you this, really," he said, "because, after all, we all live by our illusions, *but I was the one who cut your opponent.*"

"The hell you did." It was now my turn to say it.

"I realized how frightened you were," he said, "so I decided to get you out of it as quickly as I could. In that last huddle at Santelli's, I pushed through that change to 'first blood' and then, the very moment I shouted 'go' I drew that first blood by inflicting a harmless flesh wound on your opponent."

He was quiet for a moment, then said: "I thought you knew it. How on earth did you think you could cut him in his back while he was facing you?"

I was so insulted and scandalized that I promptly challenged him to a duel.

Success
Story

SOMEWHAT IN THE MANNER IN WHICH THE SAVARIN PEOPLE
label their pleasant brew "the coffier coffee," I like to think
of Laszlo Herendi, the noted motion picture producer and
discoverer of voluptuous Eva Kodaly, as the hungarianer
Hungarian. He was, I felt throughout our long friendship, the
prototype of the true Magyar, if not in the depth of his ancestral roots then certainly in the phenomenally Hungarian
quality of his accomplishments.

His success story seems to me the living confirmation of
Huxley's claim that there is the greatest practical benefit in
making a few failures early in our lives. Already before he
blossomed into a mogul of the movies, Laszlo bested Huxley
by making quite a success of his failures. He was one of the
bravest men, always cheerful and optimistic in the face of
adversities, in which he invariably perceived only the silver
linings.

I did not know him in Hungary, where his traits probably

179

would not have stood out in such glowing fashion, if only because those traits used to be quite common and widespread in our native land. But in Berlin and London, and eventually in New York and Hollywood, we became close. I enjoyed his company, mainly because it accorded me, a stranger among strangers, a sort of extraterritoriality on my own wanderings: wherever Laszlo was, he turned that particular place into a bit of Hungary.

I made his acquaintance during my salad days in Berlin where I was still a struggling newcomer to the vicissitudes of expatriate existence while he had already settled down to the art of living rather well without any visible means of support. This was, of course, a euphemism in Herendi's case. His means of support were visible in the cafés on Kurfürstendamm and in the *Weisz Csárda*, Berlin's best Hungarian restaurant. They were a handful of our fellow Hungarians, gainfully employed, who kept sustaining him with what he called "occasional loans."

This was another Herendi euphemism. He was very fussy and prudish on this score. He called it "short-term borrowing" —the financial transaction, that is, by which he procured the funds he needed—although it never was his intention to repay those loans and never the wildest hope of the lenders to get them repaid. I recall how once he complained about Jeno Rosner, a thrifty furrier he knew slightly, whose reluctant loan, he told me in bitter tone, he had indignantly refused.

"He had strings attached to it," he said.

"What strings?" I asked.

"Why, that incredible man insisted that I eventually repay the loan."

Herendi was a roly-poly little fellow, agile despite his compact bulk and alert behind a full-moon face that exuded childlike candor and purity. As fat people so often are, Laszlo was dedicated body and soul to the *dolce vita* and succeeded, with a compound of schemes (whose secret formula was his greatest asset) in persuading a group of carefully chosen compatriots that it was their patriotic obligation to finance his predilection for the best things in life. Dressed with sedate but costly elegance (custom-made suits from Knize, dazzling silk shirts from Sulka) and puffing on enormous Upmanns, he extracted tributes from willing Hungarians who, themselves, seldom indulged in the luxuries Laszlo was accustomed to. "Let us all be happy," he would remark once in a while, with Artemus Ward as his authority, "and live within our means, even if we have to borrow the money to do it with."

To rationalize his mode of life, Laszlo developed a social philosophy which he insisted was far better and simpler than any Marxian nonsense. He was quick to elaborate it whenever conversation turned to the inherent problems of capitalism, with which he carried on a Freudian love-hate affair.

"The trouble with our society is pretty well wrapped up in the silly saying," he would say, "that the world does not owe us a living. If we would only realize that, indeed, it does, we would have our Elysian fields, and *everybody* would be happy and prosperous."

Herendi's success in life was neither haphazard nor accidental. He was groomed to succeed. He was the only son of a modest but innately ambitious little neighborhood tailor who, having had his shop in a fashionable and expensive neighborhood, took in only the most elegant and costly suits to press or patch up. Whenever he ironed a pair of exquisite pants made of imported English fabric by Lahner & Sons, the town's best custom tailors, the old man would fall to brooding and visualize his chubby son grown up to wear such fine pants and enjoy all that went with them.

He realized, of course, that on the income of a little tailor shop he could not give his son the education and upbringing that would ensure his success in life. So he branched out in

business by adding two sidelines which he thought would bring
about a quick and radical improvement in his exchequer. He
went into moneylending at extraordinary interest rates; and
then also became a *lókupec,* as traders in horses were somewhat contemptuously called in Hungary.

In due course, Laszlo's father became the court-usurer of
Guido Count de Feherhazy, an extravagant young nobleman
who maintained a harem of mistresses and a stable of race
horses, mostly on loans old Herendi floated for him. While
Feherhazy was getting steadily poorer in the process, the
manysided tailor was becoming richer, until one day he began
flirting with the idea that maybe he himself could own a racing stable. He became so obsessed with the idea that next time,
when Guido de Feherhazy summoned him to the *palais* for an
urgent loan of ten thousand pengoes, the little tailor told the
young Count:

"I have a proposition, Your Excellency. Instead of *loaning*
you the ten thousand pengoes, I'll *give* them to you . . ."

"*Give* them to me?" he asked incredulously.

"Yes, sir, *give* them to you . . . provided you *give* me Villám
III."

"You must be out of your mind!" Count Guido exclaimed.
"The colt is my best three-year-old. I'm planning to enter him
at Epsom Downs."

Just then, Feherhazy was called out of the room to be given
the tragic news that Villám III had broken his leg during that
morning's workout and had to be put to sleep. The news
naturally depressed the Count but not as much as it would
have under different circumstances. Now he returned to old
Herendi and told him:

"On second thought, and since I need a spot of hard cash
more urgently than usual, I might consider parting with Villám III, provided you give me the ten thousand pengoes right
away, no strings attached."

A deal was made then and there. Old Herendi handed over the cash and the papers were signed and sealed. Then the new owner of Villám III was driven to the Feherhazy Stables and escorted to the stall that held the limp body of the celebrated thoroughbred. There was nothing the little tailor could do. He depended on the Count's good will and could not protest the sale. He drove back to town, straight to the Café Jokai, the regular hangout of loan sharks and horse traders in Budapest, and proclaimed in triumph that he had just bought Villám III from Count de Feherhazy, producing the papers to substantiate his claim.

"But to tell the truth," he told his *confrères* at usury and horse trading who quickly assembled around his table, "it was a foolish thing to do because I can ill afford such an expensive toy. Besides," he moaned, "ten thousand pengoes was a stiff price for that colt, but I had no choice. I had to humor the Count."

Old Herendi seemed downhearted in his hour of triumph, but only for a moment. Then his face lit up again.

"I just had an idea," he said, "a very good idea, at that, whereby any one of you could gain possession of Villám III for just a hundred pengoes." The startled silence that followed this statement was broken by Moe Petzall, who asked: "How?"

"I'll raffle him off," old Herendi said.

The idea struck the assembled loan sharks and *lókupecs* as truly inspired, and in no time old Herendi had sold two hundred tickets in this *ad hoc* lottery, at a hundred pengoes each. The numbers were placed in the big punch bowl the Café Jokai used only once a year, to aid in the celebration of the new year on Sylvester Nights; and Jolanka, the youngest and prettiest waitress in the establishment, was blindfolded to draw the winning number from the bowl.

"It's number fifty-seven," she announced in a voice shrill

with excitement; then Izzy Metzger yelled out, even more excitedly:

"I have fifty-seven!"

"Congratulations," old Herendi said, then drove the lucky winner, as he had been driven a few hours before, to the Feherhazy Stables—to the remains of poor Villám III.

"But this horse is dead," Metzger exclaimed.

"All right," old Herendi said in an injured tone yet soothing at the same time, "so it is dead. Here is your hundred back, Izzy, and please don't give me any more arguments."

"But how about the others?" Izzy asked meekly.

"What about them?"

"Aren't you going to give them their money back, too?"

"Why should I?" the little tailor-usurer-*lókupec* said. "They didn't win."

Later that same night, the old man related the incident to his son, the latest in a series of bedtime stories with which he taught Laszlo the tricks of success. He called this particular sutra "How to Recoup a Loss," but by then, it seemed, there was little he could teach his son.

"Why was it necessary," young Laszlo asked disapprovingly, "to give Izzy Metzger his money back?"

"Why?" asked the old man, slightly scandalized. "Because you must be *honest*, son, that's why! Remember this, Laci, you must always be *honest* if you wish to succeed."

Laszlo graduated from his father's improvised college rather abruptly when, a few years later, old Herendi was suddenly arrested on a charge of usury sworn out by Feherhazy and countless other counts. This was when Laszlo moved to Berlin, penniless and with his education not quite completed. Probably it was the memory of his father's failure as a money-lender that made him drift to the other extreme and become a professional borrower. He developed that ancient art into a modern science, with an intricate apparatus he laboriously devised to aid him in his pursuits. He had an elaborate index system with a separate card for each of his victims. Little green, blue and red metal markers on the cards showed him at a quick glance how solvent his individual clients were—the green markers designating people good for a maximum of ten marks at best; the blue markers indicating individuals good for up to fifty marks; and red markers for those delightful people who had no apparent ceiling on their generosity. Laszlo kept the cards, not alphabetically but in chronological order, with the dates of his touches meticulously entered upon the cards.

It was a formidable system of bookkeeping, especially for those pre-IBM days. It aided Laszlo immeasurably in rotating his touches and making them produce. Each afternoon when he awoke, he would consult his cards and decide whom he would approach that day for a short-term loan. On critical days, when his rent was due or he had to take out Eva Kodaly, the madcap chorine from the Metropol's revue whom he was to discover and parlay into an international movie star, Laszlo would consult only the cards which had red markers on them. On other days he was not too choosy, although it made him restive and uncomfortable when he found he was down to a succession of green markers.

I lost contact with Laszlo when once I hurt his feelings, even though unintentionally. I was sent to cover the civil war in Spain and got lost in the shuffle when a Loyalist unit I happened to be with at that time came under siege by a Moorish battalion. When the siege was lifted at last and I could return to my base in Hendaye, on the French side of the border, I found in my mail a special delivery letter postmarked Stockholm. It was from Laszlo Herendi, instructing me in no uncertain terms to wire him at once a hundred pounds sterling so that he could check out of the Grand Hotel, or else he would be arrested the next morning for what is called *"Zechprellerei"* in those parts. Although the word sounds pleasantly melodious (just try saying *"Zechprellereï"* a few times to yourself), it really means "cheating an innkeeper out of the amount due." The Swedish police in particular take a rather dim view of its practitioners, called *"Zechpreller"* or "one who shirks his score," so I could see it at once what Laszlo had been up against.

He had sent the letter to London where I then lived. It was forwarded to my wife in Budapest, waiting there for my return from the wars. She then sent it on to me at Hendaye. By the time I received it, the express missive was more than two months old, and I feared any help I could have given Laszlo would have been too late.

I worried needlessly. Laszlo had sent identical special delivery letters to every entry in his index system with red markers on their cards and received a grand total of eight hundred pounds sterling in return. It enabled him to pay off that innkeeper in Stockholm and left him enough to finance his migration to America.

Contrary to popular belief, Laszlo was not immediately successful in the United States. As a matter of fact, when I bumped into him in New York, he had to eke out a living by doing all sorts of odd chores because his credit system had broken down. Even so, at the time of our reunion, he had a couple of dollars stashed away, what was left of a five hundred dollar stipend he had received for joining a mystic, pseudo-Hindu, quasi-religious sect. Called the Hagiography Society, it had its shrine in Steinway Hall on 57th Street, in a two-room suite on the eleventh floor. The Society was supported by an elderly lady named Hortense Ballantine-Twitch, multi-millionaire widow of a pancake-mix manufacturer from Minneapolis in whose blessed memory she had established the Society and to whose inspiration she was forever burning incense, which beclouded the whole eleventh floor. In her missionary zeal, Mrs. Ballantine-Twitch advertised for converts in the *New York Journal,* offering them a hundred dollars each if and when they joined. Laszlo answered one of her ads, then persuaded Mrs. Ballantine-Twitch that *his* conversion was worth five hundred dollars.

It was inevitable that Herendi should eventually gravitate to Hollywood. Once there he revived his index-card system, what with all those Hungarians in the movie colony who remembered him fondly from the good old days in Berlin. Yet when only a few months after his arrival I looked him up in the Bel Air Hotel, where he lived in his old style, I found he was using the index cards just to stay in form, not actually needing the revenue they yielded.

"I have a job," he told me with unconcealed disgust.

"Where do you work?" I asked. I had spent several days and nights with him by then, but never saw him taking time out for his job.

"I don't work," he said. "I'm a consultant to Joe Pastor."

"Pastor?" I asked incredulously. "Isn't he the big cheese at Paramus Pictures? Why would Pastor need *you* as a consultant?"

He didn't seem to be hurt by the question, because he merely said: "I'm supposed to tell him whether a picture of his is good or bad."

"I don't get it."

"You know what a candid man I am," he explained. "Don't I always tell the unvarnished truth to everybody, no matter how it hurts?"

"Yes I know," I said. "You are an unvarnished S.O.B."

He had set views on everything and dispensed them whether solicited or not. He would tell Ilona Halley, "I'm afraid, darling, you're getting wrinkled around the neck"; and ask Otto Preminger, "Why don't you learn to speak English?" It was a mixture of frankness and abuse, but somehow, in a world addicted to shameless flattery, Laszlo not only got away with it but actually prospered from it.

Joe Pastor was a big shot, to be sure, but he was rampant with inferiority complexes. He was surrounded by yes-men who never dared to contradict him or speak frankly to him. When Herendi showed up in Hollywood, Pastor—a barefoot boy from a small hamlet in Hungary—hired him to tell the truth to his face.

"Whenever I finish a picture, I'll sneak-preview it solely for you, boy," Pastor told Laszlo. "Then you tell me whether it's good or bad. Don't be afraid to tell me if it stinks. I want the goddam truth! That's all. I'll put you on the Paramus payroll as my consultant with . . . let me see . . . five hundred bucks a week."

That was eleven months before.

Herendi was getting his check every week, sent to him in the Bel Air Hotel, but though Joe Pastor was finishing one picture after another, he had never called in Laszlo to tell him the unvarnished truth. It was too good to be true. But it was true. It was the softest job in Hollwood.

Then one smoggy morning, when Herendi returned to Bel Air from a party in Eva Kodaly's bungalow in Santa Monica, the night clerk stopped him. "Mr. Pastor has called several times," he said. "He wants you to call him, no matter how late."

Laszlo called Pastor's Gladstone number at his home and heard the mogul yell at him: "Where the hell were you, Laci? I've been looking for you everywhere on the Strip. Listen, boy. This is it! I've got *Tomorrow Is Yesterday* in the can and I want you to see it first thing in the morning, just you and me. I want the unvarnished truth!"

"I don't know about you, Joe, but I am wide awake," Herendi said, showing some zeal for work for the first time in his life. "How about looking at the picture right away!"

"Okay, boy," Pastor said, "it's a deal. It's ideal because there won't be a goddam soul in the whole goddam studio. A real, honest-to-goodness sneak preview, boy, if there ever was one! Meet me in my office in an hour. I'll get a projectionist in the meantime to roll it for us."

It was a little after five o'clock in the morning when Joe Pastor and Laszlo Herendi entered the executive projection room at Paramus Pictures and settled down in a couple of overstuffed proscenium chairs to view what Pastor fondly hoped would be the Paramus epic of the year. *Tomorrow Is Yesterday* was billed as one of those super-colossal productions and from its success Pastor expected to become executive producer at Paramus.

Laszlo suddenly realized he had made a horrible mistake when he suggested that they sneak the preview into this dawn. He was getting a hang-over and there seemed to be nothing in the plot of *Tomorrow Is Yesterday* that would have kept his eyes open. While Pastor slid to the edge of his chair and watched the picture avidly leaning forward, Laszlo reclined in his big chair, then slowly but surely went to sleep.

Yesterday was already tomorrow when the picture ground to an end. The screen went dark at 8:27 a.m. and Pastor now nudged Herendi in the twilight of the projection room to get the unvarnished truth from him.

"Na?" the producer asked hopefully. "What do you say, boy?"

Herendi came to life somewhat slowly. He suppressed a yawn and pressed his numb arms against his side, trying to shake himself awake, but he was still half asleep when he said:

"It stinks."

This briefest of all critical appraisals in the whole history of Hollywood took Joe Pastor's breath away. For a moment he could merely stare at Laszlo in the semi-darkness, hoping that he did not hear him right. He was almost solicitous when he said:

"What did you say, boy?"

"I said it stinks."

Pastor switched on the ceiling lights with a Napoleonic gesture, stepped into the aisle and pulled himself up to his total length of five feet five. Then, in a tone that had in it all the wrath and anguish his ancestors had accumulated when building pyramids for the Pharaohs, he said in a muffled voice, to keep things from the projectionist:

"You lousy little ingrate, how dare you? I paid you for the unvarnished truth, not for your opinion! *You* stink, you hear me? You're fired! And get out of here before I call the studio cops!"

That was when Laszlo Herendi's phenomenal success story really began. The story of the sneak preview leaked out and when *Tomorrow Is Yesterday* became poison at the box office, Hollywood took notice of Laszlo Herendi.

The last I heard of him was that he had replaced Joe Pastor as production chief at Paramus and was looking for someone to tell *him* the unvarnished truth.

Strictly from Hungary

THERE IS ONE THEORY AS FIRMLY ESTABLISHED AMONG HUN-
garians as Einstein's theory of relativity is among physicists and
mathematicians. But there is nothing relative about the Hungarian theory. It asserts boldly and bluntly that *"Mindenki
magyar"*—everybody is Hungarian.

I have the sneaking suspicion that everybody is, because I
myself had several opportunities in my wanderings to see the
validity of the theory. I had what I regard as the definitive
proof when I once visited a small place called Old Meldrum
way up in Scotland and lost my way in the quaint town. I
stopped a bonny stranger in the street and asked him in English with a distinct Hungarian brogue:

"Pardon me, sir, but would you tell me please how I could
best get to the railroad station, if any?"

He told me, too—in flawless Hungarian, because the bonny
stranger I happened to pick at random also happened to be a
Hungarian. I had similar experiences in a dispensary in Aden,

191

in a monastery in Jerusalem, in the office of a slave trader in Djibouti, in nightclubs from Rio to Shanghai, at St. Peter's in Rome and in a reindeer-hide tannery in Kiruna, a town in Lapland above the Arctic Circle.

Everybody *is* Hungarian!

By now it should not come as a surprise to you that the famous Houdini was also a Hungarian. And if you are a devotee of the "Late, Late Show," you undoubtedly know that Dracula was a native of Transylvania which in turn used to be part of historic Hungary. But would you believe me if I told you that Leslie Howard, the most British of all actors, was a Hungarian, too? Well, he was, as was the late Queen Mary of England, and even proud of it. Whenever that great lady happened to meet a Hungarian, she never failed to mention that she was of Magyar stock. You see? Everybody is *Hungarian!*

Once in Geneva, during the thirties, the Foreign Ministers of Czechoslovakia, Rumania and Yugoslavia met behind closed doors at the League of Nations to discuss some diplomatic move against their common adversary, Hungary. Their conference bogged down because none of the Foreign Ministers seemed to know a language the other could understand. The impasse was ended when Milan Hodza, Foreign Minister of Czechoslovakia, asked his colleagues: "Why don't we hold this conference in Hungarian?" No sooner said than done. Hungarian was the only foreign language each of them spoke fluently because they used to be Hungarians before the *denouement* of World War I made them a Czech, a Rumanian and a Yugoslav respectively.

This basic theory was carried a bit further by my friend Eugene Fodor, the genius behind the brilliant travel guides named after him. According to Gene, everybody is, not only from Hungary, but more specifically from Losoncz, a lively city in old Hungary where the Fodors had their ancestral

home. For all I know, Gene could be right! Not too long ago
in New York, I attended the *vernissage* of a gifted lady painter
in a gallery on Madison Avenue, and when I was introduced
to her, she told me:

"Judging by your name you must be a Hungarian, and
so am I."

"Well," I responded lightly, "it doesn't surprise me, because
everybody is Hungarian. What's more," I quipped, "according
to my good friend Gene Fodor, everybody is from Losoncz."

The talented artist paled as she said in a whisper:

"I don't know if *everybody* is from Losoncz . . . *but I am.*"

Natives and to the manner born, Hungarians enchant some,
intrigue or irritate others. They definitely rubbed some of the
greatest Anglo-Saxon poets the wrong way. Thus the Merry
Wives of Windsor were hardly off to a spirited start, when
Shakespeare seemed to have been seized by a sudden compul-
sion to vent his feelings about Hungarians. Right then and
there in the third scene of Act I, he made Koming exclaim:
"O base Hungarian wight! wilt though the spigot wield?" I
personally consider it a rather uncalled-for remark, especially
because we Hungarians are always only too pleased to wield
the spigot, whatever it is.

Ezra Pound, for reasons of his own, also thought fit to dep-
recate Hungarians in a poem he titled—with sly innuendo, I
presume—*An Immorality.* Pound insisted that he would rather
have his sweet, though rose-leaves die of grieving, than do
high deeds in Hungary to pass all men's believing.

George Bernard Shaw, in a similar mood, made one Zoltan
Karpathy, a mercurial Hungarian, a villain in *Pygmalion.* Alan
Jay Lerner then went a step further in his musical adaptation
of the Shavian masterpiece, saying of poor Zoltan in *My Fair
Lady* something to the effect: "He is a guest from Budapest.
I never saw a ruder pest."

Whether they are base wights and rude pests, or charming,

entertaining vagabonds, Hungarians are here to stay—permanent fixtures of the landscape, just any landscape at all. As for myself, although unhappily I am not from Losoncz, I am rather proud to be from Hungary, for what other race or nation has such a breath-taking range in the accomplishments of its sons and daughters? Where is the people that produced a man who became the father of the H-bomb and a woman who became the mother of the Gabor sisters?

Hate them or love them, you can't ignore them, and what is worse, you can't do without them. Just try to think of contemporary music without Bela Bartok and Zoltan Kodaly, without Eugene Ormandy, Fritz Reiner, George Szell, George Sebastian and George Solti. Would there now be an atomic age without Edward Teller, Jeno Wigner, George de Hevesy, Leo Szilard, John von Neumann; and even worse, would there be a ball-point pen without a Hungarian named Biro who invented it? We might still be without vitamin C had not Albert von Szent-Gyorgyi discovered it; and without riboflavin, but for Pal Gyorgy who succeeded in isolating it.

Music could not enjoy its current popularity in our homes if Peter C. Goldmark had not invented the long-playing record; and the world would not be safe from diphtheria had not Bela Schick devised the test to determine susceptibility to the dread disease.

And Hollywood? What would it be without Adolf Zukor and George Cukor, without Mike Curtiz and Tony Curtis? And what would Jayne Mansfield be without Mickey Hargitay?

Do you still doubt that *everybody* is Hungarian?

They run the mile in under four minutes, find long-lost Lincolniana in dusty New England garrets, write hit plays for the Spanish stage, desalt sea water, marry oily emirs in Saudi Arabia, harness the energy of the sun, dehydrate mushroom soup, paint heroic murals for the United Nations, come and go, restive and active forever.

It isn't easy to keep track of these gregarious and ubiqui-tous people, but fortunately there is in New York a dedicated Magyar historian who collects famous Hungarians like Billy Rose collecting Picassos, both genuine and bogus. Our his-torian keeps count of us, records our achievements and lists us diligently in a roster that keeps growing by leaps and bounds. He is as elated when he stumbles upon another Hun-garian who made good as Lord Rothschild, the late great entomologist, must have been when he found another species of the *Blatta orientalis* for his famous cockroach collection.

Just the other day, when I happened to bump into him in the reading room of the New York Public Library, I thought to detect a special glow on his erudite face. I was right. He was aglow.

"Guess what?" he said.

"You found that warm water was invented by a Hungarian," I said.

"No," he said sharply. "But I have discovered that George Washington was a Hungarian."

"You're kidding!"

"This is far too serious a matter to kid about," he shot back sternly. "According to Mabel Thacher Rosemary Washburn, the well-known American genealogist, the authenticated line-age of George Washington could hitherto be traced only to John Washington of Tuwhitfield in Lancashire, England, who lived about the middle of the fifteenth century. Before that everything went blank! But now, I have . . ."

"You mean to tell me," I interrupted him in some excite-ment, "that you have now . . ."

"Yes," he said with proud finality. "I have established be-yond the shadow of a doubt that the Father of Our Adopted Country was also a descendant of our beloved Native Land.

He is a lineal descendant of our own Szent Istvan, better known hereabouts as St. Stephen, first king of Hungary, who reigned from 1001 to 1038."

"You don't say."

"But I most definitely do. Stephen married the German princess Gisella and in association with her sired Agatha, who in turn married Edward I. Among their issue was Margaret—St. Margaret of Scotland—who married Malcolm III, son of Duncan I . . . and so on, down the line to Henry I, youngest son of William the Conqueror. Henry's great-great-great-granddaughter, Margaret Butler, married Lawrence, son of our John Washington of Tuwhitfield. Do you follow me?"

"I am afraid I don't," I said. "As a matter of fact, I lost you somewhere at the issue of the first Edward."

"Of course," he said with scholarly condescension. "But I have here a genealogical table in which I demonstrate George Washington's Hungarian origin, without the shadow of a doubt."

He pulled a sheet of paper from his briefcase and handed me a neatly drawn family tree which I propose to reproduce here without any further ado:

Well, there you have it, black on white: George Washington, of all people—or Vasington György, to give his name its proper Hungarian sequence and spelling—strictly from Hungary.

THE END

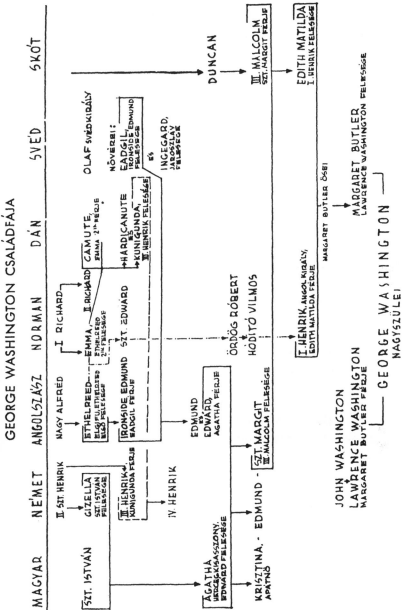

GEORGE WASHINGTON CSALÁDFÁJA

John's All-Purpose Hungarian Recipe

(This recipe is based on the premise that all Hungarian dishes, or at least all Hungarian meat stews, are basically variations on a theme.)

PHASE I: FRY THE ONIONS.

The first step is to fry the onions. Dice 2 large onions. Fry in fat appropriate to the meat (lard for pork, goosefat for poultry, either of these or butter or suet for beef or veal). The trick is that you want the onions to begin to brown—caramelize—which brings out their sweetness, dries them out, and gets rid of the oniony aftertaste. If the temperature is allowed to drop too much, the onions will turn to mush before they caramelize. To avoid this, use a pan that retains heat. Cast iron or enameled cast iron takes a long time to change temperature. The heavier the better. Then get it as hot as possible, which means bring the fat to just below the temperature at which it starts to smoke (when the first hints of smoke appear, throw in the onions). Solid fats—goosefat, lard, butter, Crisco, suet—start to smoke at a higher temperature than liquid fats (that makes sense, since they melt into liquid from a solid at a higher temperature).

Add about a tablespoon of salt, sprinkle with a good hit of pepper, and fry at medium-high heat. The fat is what keeps the onions from burning, so there needs to be a good bit of it (I start with about 4-6 tablespoons and add more if it looks like things are sticking too much). You wind up cooking the water out of them, so eventually they should be golden brown with very few bubbles, just fat and onions left in the pan.

Variant: *Peppers*. Almost all Hungarian dishes except *Szekely Gulyas* require peppers as well as onions. No peppers for *Szekey Gulyas*! I chop the peppers after I throw the onions into the pan and throw the peppers in with the frying onions as soon as they are all chopped. This gives the pan a chance to heat back up and the onions a chance to start to caramelize before the peppers add their water and make it harder to get everything to brown. The peppers, too, should cook out their water and begin to brown around the edges.

198

Variant: *Root vegetables*. Before adding peppers, consider adding a couple of handfuls of finely chopped carrots and perhaps 1/3 or 1/2 that amount of chopped parsnips. These should cook down to almost nothing before it's all done, so get them well softened while sautéing. The effect is to sweeten the sauce somewhat, and make it richer.

Variant: *Apple*. I add a thinly sliced whole apple (something tart, usually Granny Smith) to the onions and peppers. Start to peel after you throw in the peppers, core it, slice it translucently thin, throw it in.

Variant: *Mushrooms*. Not a very Hungarian *gulyas* ingredient, but mushrooms absorb the flavor of whatever they are cooked with, pretty intensively, so they are an interesting addition to any flavorful stew. Here the trick is to cook the water out of them before putting them in the stew. They should be quartered or sliced, and sautéed on very high heat until all the water cooks out but not until they brown, and then added to the pot once the peppers and onions are starting to brown.

Variant: *Caraway seeds*. You can, and probably should, throw a tablespoon or less of caraway seeds in with the onions, peppers, and apple (not for *Szekely Gulyas*, though for reasons that become obvious).

PHASE II: BROWN THE MEAT.

The next step is to sear the meat so that it stays moist as it stews. It doesn't matter what the meat is. Cut the meat into 1-inch chunks, unless you're using a whole chicken, then cut it up into eight pieces, dry the meat, and rub with salt, pepper, and some form of garlic (crushed actually works least well because it burns easily; powdered, granulated, or garlic salt works well). Be generous with all three parts of the rub.

Remove the vegetables from the fat (let the fat drain back into the pot), and crank up the heat again. In relatively small batches, sear the meat so that it crusts at the edges. Let it sit for a bit without stirring or it won't brown. Then turn and scrape it a bit till it's browned all around. Again, unless the heat is high, the meat will start to simmer in its own juices, which is sort of the opposite of what you want.

When all the meat is done, deglaze the pan of the brown/black stuff that's stuck to the bottom. You can use water to do this, say, about 1/2 cup. Scrape the bottom as the water boils, and let it boil vigorously until it pretty much all has evaporated.

Variant: *Deglazing liquid*. I actually use Tokaji or some other sweet dessert wine. But you can use Port (I use white Port) or apple cider. I also add the juice of about 1/2 lemon (be careful not to let the seeds fall in; they turn sour when they cook).

PHASE III: STEW IT.

Throw the meat, onions, peppers, etc. back into the pot with the fat and add the paprika. I use a vast amount (about 1/2 cup) of the sweetest Hungarian paprika I can find. Mix it around until the paprika dissolves. If you don't mix it, it will burn in the fat. Bring the temperature down to the lowest simmer you can get and put a cover on it.

Variant: *Hot Paprika*. In addition to the sweet paprika, I add about 1/2 teaspoon of hot paprika. You can always add more later if you want it spicy.

Variant: *Szekely Gulyas*. *Szekely Gulyas* is a pork *gulyas* with sauerkraut. Once the pork is simmering, it's time to start thinking about the sauerkraut. The question here is, "How sour do you like it?" I like it not very sour. I buy fresh kraut from a Hungarian butcher or a place that sells fresh pickles, and I rinse it with cold water until it tastes right. You should make sure that it's still at least a little sour, that's sort of the point. Then simmer it in a separate pot (to get it warm and soft), with about 2 tablespoons of caraway seeds mixed in. The balance between kraut and meat is entirely up to you; use anywhere from equal amounts (by weight, uncooked) to twice as much meat as kraut.

Variant: *Tomatoes*. While it is simmering, you can add tomatoes: 1 can or less of whole Italian-style plum tomatoes, mushed up, or 1 similar-sized can of crushed tomatoes, or as much thick tomato paste as you feel like, or two to three fresh tomatoes, or whatever you'd like. This is entirely a matter of personal taste. Tomatoes can add sweetness, intensity, and color, depending on what you use and how much. My mother always used to sneak in a couple of tablespoons of thickened paste. I toss in a fresh tomato or two if I have a couple that are very ripe, and when I cook in volume I'll toss in a large canful for bulk and flavor. Start with none; experiment to see whether you want to add any.

PHASE IV: FINISH THE SAUCE.

Let the stew simmer for at least a couple of hours, until the meat stops being tough and chewy. Be patient, it will eventually get flaky and soft. When it does, you're almost done. How you finish the sauce depends on what you want it to be when you're done.

Variant: *Szekely Gulyas*. Basically, all you have to do now is drain the kraut and combine it with the meat. Stir it around, add a bit more (2 to 4 tablespoons) sweet paprika so that the kraut will take on a rosy red color, and simmer them together for 30 minutes or so, very low heat, stirring occasionally so it doesn't burn. When you serve it, add sour cream to taste and stir it around so the color turns a creamy red. About 1 cup should do it. You can put more sour cream on the table with it, as well as sweet and hot paprikas. A variant within the variant: You can add sliced sausage during this final heating phase while the meat and kraut are together. *Debrecen* (a Hungarian sausage) or *kolbasz* or any sausage you feel like, about 1/2- to 1-inch-thick rounds. You can also add another apple, finely diced, but then be sure to keep the dish simmering until the apple turns soft and indistinguishably mushy.

Variant: *Gulyas* soup. Real *gulyas* is a thin beef soup, more sharp than sweet. If that's what you're aiming for, add some beef or veal or even chicken stock to thin it down to watery consistency, and add hot paprika to taste. You can boil some potatoes in with it and some carrots and parsnips and turnips if you want. If you're going to add these vegetables, don't let the meat get too soft in phase III before you add them, since you'll be cooking it for about another hour after the vegetables get tossed in. Serve with tiny dumplings cooked in the *gulyas*, a dollop of sour cream (about 1 teaspoon per bowl) and sprinkle with a dash of hot paprika on top.

Variant: *Goulash*. Actually, in Hungarian, a *pörkölt*. At the end of phase III, that's pretty much what you have. Make sure the sauce is hearty and flavorful. If not, remove the meat and boil it down (you can also add paprika) to get a dense, intense sauce. It will be thinned a bit by the cream, so you really want it intense. When it's to taste, serve with sour cream and hot and sweet paprikas on the side. A variant within the variant: there is no defensible reason not to add 1 cup of heavy cream at the very end. Mix it in.

VARIANT: *Paprikas*. *Paprikas* sauce is a smooth creamy sauce. Take the meat out of the stew and get the sauce to the same intense place described above for goulash. There's no turning back; however intense you get it here, that's the most it will ever be again, so make sure you're happy with it before going on. Then throw the onions, peppers, etc. into a food processor with whatever sauce travels with them, and puree them down into a smooth paste (if you have added mushrooms, it sort of ruins them to puree them, so I'd leave it as a goulash if you've got mushrooms in it). Throw the puree back into the sauce. (Do it slowly, so that you get the right texture and taste to suit you.) Add the meat back in. (This will thin the sauce a bit because the meat juices will have come out while it was sitting there.) Add 1 cup of heavy cream (or less, to taste). Stir. Serve with sour cream. I put a dollop on each serving (about 2 tablespoons), and let the people mix it in themselves, or you can just serve it on the side.

Final Notes: Serve with some form of noodle or dumpling. You can always correct flavor by playing with any of the following at any stage (in diminishing order of rationality): salt, sweet paprika, hot paprika, sweet wine (Tokaji or port), lemon juice, garlic powder, apple cider.

Made in the USA
Monee, IL
27 August 2019